AIR SHOW

AIR SHOW

THE DRAMA & SPEED OF PRECISION FLYING

Philip Handleman, Mike Jerram,
Nigel Moll, Norman Pealing,
Philip Wallick

MILITARY PRESS
New York

© Osprey Publishing Limited

This 1990 edition published by
Military Press, New York, and
distributed by Crown Publishers, Inc.,
225 Park Avenue South, New York,
New York 10003.

Printed and bound in Hong Kong

ISBN 0–517–01221–9

hgfedcba

Compiled and edited by
Richard Widdows

Designed by Janette Widdows
and Melanie Clitheroe

[The material in this book previously
appeared in the Osprey publications *Airshow
USA* (Philip Handleman), *EAA Oshkosh*
and *Reno: Air Racing Unlimited* (Nigel
Moll), *Reno 2* and *Warbirds* (Mike Jerram),
American Warbirds (Norman Pealing) and
Reno Gold (Philip Wallick)]

CONTENTS

TITLE PAGE The Steve Hinton/John Maloney *Super Corsair*, based at the Planes of Fame Museum in California, banks on its way to Gold victory at the National Championship Air Races in 1985. Hinton, Unlimited winner at the helm of *Red Baron* back in 1978, clocked over 438 mph in the final to set a new Reno race record. [*Mike Jerram*]

OPPOSITE This better not be for real . . . a replica Zero puts in a strafing run as part of the reenactment of the Japanese attack on Pearl Harbor at the annual Confederate Air Force show at Harlingen in 1987. [*Philip Handleman*]

OVERLEAF An array of colorful biplanes from across the United States decorate Bartlesville, Oklahoma at the National Biplane's Association's first annual Fly-In during the 1987 season. [*Philip Handleman*]

PHILIP HANDLEMAN has enjoyed a lifelong love affair with aviation. A pilot for nearly 20 years, he owns and flies a vintage military trainer – the open-cockpit Boeing Stearman biplane. His published work includes a wide range of articles for numerous aviation magazines and the book *Airshow USA*. He is also an award-winning film-maker whose documentaries have been seen on many public television stations in the United States and distributed internationally.

MIKE JERRAM's earliest recollection of warbirds is of watching Fleet Air Arm Fireflies, Sea Furies and Sea Hornets landing at Lee-on-Solent in Hampshire,

England. Although his work as a freelance aviation writer and photographer now brings him into contact with every kind of flying machine from microlights to the Space Shuttle, he has a particular passion for vintage aircraft and warbirds and has spent many years photographing them. Mike, who lives and works on the south coast of England, is contributing editor of the British general aviation magazine *Pilot* and an assistant compiler of *Jane's All the World's Aircraft*.

NIGEL MOLL began his journalistic career with *Flight International* in London, but his evocative writing, sharp reporting and outstanding photography have

graced the pages of the New York-based *Flying* magazine for over a decade. An enthusiastic private pilot with single, multi-engined and helicopter ratings who has flown more than 50 different types of aircraft, his prefered form of transport is a Beech Bonanza.

NORMAN PEALING began taking pictures before he entered the Royal Air Force in 1958, but his photographic portfolio was not allowed to expand into aviation subjects in the days when RAF Marham and Wittering were stuffed full of Valiant nuclear bombers. In 1965 he joined the British Aircraft Corporation (BAC), and began making sales and publicity films to promote all the company's products. By 1983 he chose to leave what had become the Weybridge Division of British Aerospace (BAe) to form his own company at Fairoaks Airport in Surrey. Aviation Image specializes in aviation photography and film and video production for advertising, sales support, public relations, publishing and television.

PHILIP WALLICK is a professional freelance photographer based at Chico, California. His company offers a full range of specialist services including multi-media production, video production and air-to-air photography.

SHOWTIME

LEFT The Eagles team up briefly at Reno 82 with the two Pitts S-2As of the Ray-Ban Reds (Rod Ellis and Bill Cowan), Canada's only civilian aerobatic team. [*Nigel Moll*]

BELOW It's an understatement to say that Eagles team members like to fly close: they almost collide here during a 1987 performance. [*Philip Handleman*]

ABOVE Between the heats at Reno, it's airshow performers galore. Here the Eagles paint the sky in 1987. [*Philip Handleman*]

RIGHT The Eagles, in person, are wingmen Tom Poberezny (left), Gene Soucy (center) and leader Charlie Hillard. Their airplanes are 260-hp Christen Eagles, perfectly suited to the task. Charlie Hillard, a former world aerobatic champion with over 30 years' experience in aerobatics, is a businessman with an automobile sales organization; Tom Poberezny, equally well known for his untiring efforts at the Experimental Aircraft Association, flies right wing; and Gene Soucy, an airline pilot, was reared on aerobatics. [*Nigel Moll*]

BELOW During opposing solos and crossovers it appears that the airplanes actually touch each other. [*Philip Handleman*]

ABOVE Jim Mynning lands his Piper Cub on 'the world's smallest aircraft carrier' at Oshkosh. [*Nigel Moll*]

ABOVE LEFT Earl Cherry and *General Smoke* laying another trail at Oshkosh. The smoke is produced by injecting oil into the exhaust pipe, where it ignites. Nobody does it more billowing than Cherry and his Stearman. [*Nigel Moll*]

LEFT Earl and Paula Cherry and *General Smoke* in full flatulence. The world's biggest aviation event would hardly be complete without an airshow, so each afternoon heads crank skyward while some of the best known pilots in the business go through their routines. Like the rest of the workforce at Oshkosh, they are unpaid volunteers who do it for love and for the honor of performing before a massive crowd of aviation people. [*Nigel Moll*]

LEFT AND BELOW LEFT Some 48 hours after these pictures were taken the legendary 'Professor' Art Scholl was dead, lost in the crash of a Pitts Special during a movie filming sequence off the California coast. Scholl, who had a PhD in aeronautics, delighted Reno 85 crowds with his spectacular, pyrotechnic Super Chipmunk routine and his crazy flying in a Super Cub in Saturday's gusts, hovering on the breeze and making unbelievable flat turns in front of the grandstands. His dog Aileron was a constant companion. [*Mike Jerram*]

BELOW Jim Mynning flies while Eddie Green climbs aboard from a speeding Buick at Oshkosh in 1984. The EAA is in dairyland, Wisconsin, beside Lake Winnebago, a holy place where airplane people gather by the hundreds of thousands in late July for the biggest aviation event on earth. In recent years, however, there has been a growing rivalry between the EAA show and that put on at Harlingen, Texas, by the Confederate Air Force. [*Nigel Moll*]

OVERLEAF Eddie Andreini thrilled everyone at the 23rd annual West Coast Antique Fly-In and Air Show at Watsonville, California in 1987 with an amazing routine in his highly modified Stearman. Horsepower was more than doubled with the installation of a Pratt & Whitney 450-hp engine. The cockpit was fully enclosed by a specially manufactured bubble canopy. The already durable aircraft was further stressed for high G loads. Contorted smoke trails in the sky are Andreini's trademark. [*Philip Handleman*]

BELOW When not flying his open cockpit biplane, Jimmy Franklin is zooming through the skies in his ominous looking Aerostar. Dubbed *Starship Pride*, the airplane is the centerpiece of an airshow act specially devised for children. One of Franklin's partners on the flight line announces over the loudspeaker that the aircraft is piloted by Zar, a benevolent knight from the imaginary planet Zufrinia, who seeks support for his efforts to free his countrymen from dictatorial rule. [*Philip Handleman*]

LEFT Duck! Here comes Leo! Aerobatic champion Leo Loudenslager can do just about anything in his super agile Bud Light. Here he performs an inverted ribbon at Oshkosh in 1987. [*Philip Handleman*]

RIGHT At a more comfortable altitude over Wittman Airfield, Loudenslager brings off a knife-edge pass. [*Philip Handleman*]

BELOW A thrilling moment at Oshkosh—four wingwalkers at once! From left to right: Gene and Cheryl Rae Littlefield, Bob and Ruth Blankenship, Bill Barber and Eddie Green, Bob and Pat Wagner. No other flying event evokes as tremendous an outpouring of enthusiasm for aviation as the Experimental Aircraft Association's annual fly-in. The week-long Oshkosh extravaganza draws upwards of 800,000 spectators. Behind the ever-expanding EAA Museum is a quiet refuge—an airport within an airport. Pioneer Airport is an EAA creation, devised to resemble a 1920s airstrip and home to a panoply of gentle old ragwings, many of which are maintained in flying condition. On summer weekends, the flyable antiques can be seen taking to the sky via Pioneer Airport's tiny grass runway. [*Philip Handleman*]

SHOWTIME

A quiet interlude for one of the wingwalking Stearmans at Oshkosh. The Wisconsin town is now the headquarters of the Experimental Aircraft Association, as well as the venue for its annual fly-in and convention, with the opening of the EAA Aviation Center and Air Museum. Operated by the EAA's Aviation Foundation, the museum contains some 80 aircraft. [*Philip Handleman*]

ABOVE LEFT Wayne 'Walt' Pierce rattles a lazy Florida sky in his souped-up Stearman *Ol' Smokey*. Accompanied in wild formation by a partner in an identically decked out Stearman, Walt's airshow act was a popular attraction at the 13th annual Experimental Aircraft Association Sun 'n Fun Fly-In. [*Philip Handleman*]

LEFT Deceptively quiet during a balmy afternoon, the Stearmans of the Red Baron formation aerobatic team

await their turn to roar impressively over the anticipatory Sun 'n Fun crowds at Lakeland, Florida. Altogether there are four look-alike Stearmans that comprise the Red Baron team. It's unusual, and exciting, to see a formation aerobatic team of such number employing the bulky Stearman. [*Philip Handleman*]

ABOVE The all-black Red Baron team strut their aerobatic stuff in 1987. [*Philip Handleman*]

ABOVE Eliot Cross dives for speed in a highly modified Waco during an airshow interlude. [*Philip Handleman*]

ABOVE RIGHT Hold on – loop coming up! Jimmy Franklin tears up the sky with one of the world's leading wingwalkers, Johnny Kazian. [*Philip Handleman*]

RIGHT The two wingwalking Wacos of Jimmy Franklin being pushed ever so delicately to the Reno flight line in 1987. [*Philip Handleman*]

LEFT, RIGHT AND BELOW Californian Frank Sanders flew his Sea Fury T.20 fitted with wingtip smoke generators for airshow work. He not only painted pretty pictures in the sky with his smoke-belching airplane, but used it to give graphic demonstrations of the dangers of wingtip vortices. Sanders re-engined a two-seat Sea Fury with a 4000 hp Pratt & Whitney R-4360-28 'Corncob' engine. Named *Dreadnought* and flown by General Dynamics test pilot Neil Anderson, who is more usually seen in the sci-fi cockpit of an F-16 Fighting Falcon, the Sea Fury won the 1983 Reno Unlimited Class championship at a race speed of 425 mph. It is also featured on pages 160–3. Frank Sanders was killed in May 1990 when the Lockheed T-33 jet trainer *Red Knight*, in which he was giving a demonstration for members of the aviation press, crashed over New Mexico. [*Photographs by Mike Jerram*]

Above Two dirty passes, side by side: an extraordinary view of one of the many remarkable manouvers performed by the US Navy's Blue Angels air demonstration team, flying F/A-18 Hornets. They also appear on pages 238–9. [*Philip Handleman*]

Above right A sure way to get an airshow crowd's attention – allow two military team aircraft to fly at each other with a high closure rate and to bank away from each other at just the right moment. The

Snowbirds seem to enjoy producing multiple heart palpitations among the spectators for they perform this stunt numerous times during their routine. The Canadian team is also featured on pages 230–3 and page 240. [*Philip Handleman*]

Right The Blue Angels double farval: two F/A-18s in the formation roll inverted so that half the formation flies positive while the remainder flies upside down. [*Philip Handleman*]

SHOWTIME

A star of the 1984 airshow season was Burt Rutan's *Voyager* which, with just ten flights logged, visited Oshkosh in July from its Mojave home base. Aboard were two people – Dick Rutan (Burt's brother) and Jeana Yeager – intending to fly non-stop and unrefueled round the world to break the distance record of 12,532 miles set by a B-52H in 1962. In fact they would nearly double that: in 9 days, 3 minutes

and 44 seconds, from 14–23 December 1986, the couple flew their specially constructed aircraft 25,012 miles out of Edwards Air Force Base, averaging 115.8 mph. With a wingspan of 110 feet and capable of carrying fuel weighing 8934 lb, *Voyager* took over two years and 22,000 man-hours to build. She now resides in the National Air and Space Museum in Washington DC. [*Photographs by Nigel Moll*]

TOP LEFT Robert A. 'Bob' Hoover taught himself aerobatics at the age of 16. Since then, he has become probably the most watched pilot in history, attending all Reno Air Races in his dual role as Unlimited starter and safety pilot and airshow performer. Hoover and the yellow Rockwell International Mustang are inseparable, while his aerobatic routine in a stock Shrike Commander (right) has become one of the most famous acts in aviation history. Much of his display in the general-aviation twin is made with both engines shut down, including the falling-leaf approach and landing. [*Nigel Moll*]

ABOVE Hoover seems to pop up at just about every major airshow in the United States. While the typical airshow pilot may be satisfied to handle a lone warbird or high performance aircraft, he flies a stable of them. Having served as a test pilot for North American Aviation, he fittingly flies airplanes with roots in that company. From his T-28, crew members watch the airshow in 1987. [*Philip Handleman*]

LEFT 'Gentlemen, you have a race!' With these words uttered over the radio in his famous Mustang *Old Yeller*, Bob Hoover, by Reno tradition, starts the Unlimited heats as the aircraft thunder down the chute that leads them into the pylon course. He then pulls up to orbit high over the course like a guardian angel, ready to swoop alongside anyone calling a 'Mayday', sometimes handling as many as five emergencies at a time with calming, cooling words of often life-saving advice. [*Philip Handleman*]

RIGHT When the Reno spectators look up and see a Sabreliner business jet doing aerobatics they don't have to read the big green letters on the wings to know it must be Bob Hoover, now with Evergreen International. [*Philip Handleman*]

BELOW 'Bob' Hoover – World War 2 combat veteran, former test pilot, peripatetic airshow performer – streaks across the obliging Oshkosh sky in 1987. As part of his routine in the Shrike Commander, he performs a slow roll after intentionally shutting down an engine. [*Philip Handleman*]

BEAUTIFUL BYGONES

The standard of workmanship in this restored 1934 Stinson SR-5E won its owner/restorer, Tom Laurie, the Grand Champion Antique Award in 1984. Laurie, a lifelong aeromodeller, is not a licensed pilot, but he spotted the airplane in the back of a hangar at FlaBob Airport, Rubidoux, California, in 1974 and spent a decade rebuilding it from ruin to its current condition. Some of the immaculate specimens appearing in these pages are probably in better shape than when they were new; all of them reflect in their gleaming finishes an extraordinary amount of care and attention by their owners. Most are faithful to every detail of the original: to sit in and to fly one is to enter a vanished world of polished wood, big instruments and few of them, with not a glow-winkie or plastic gismo in sight. [*Nigel Moll*]

BEAUTIFUL BYGONES

BELOW AND RIGHT A superb Cessna 195 pictured at Oshkosh in 1984. In spite of its predilection for discarding the old in the name of progress, America has a deep respect for some pieces of its history. Aviation's past, like that of America, is comparatively recent and, thanks to restorers and enthusiasts, it's very much alive. [*Nigel Moll*]

BELOW RIGHT An 'antique' 1940 Waco UPF 7, owned by Bill Amundson and Dick Peterson; power comes from a 220-hp Continental R670 engine. An antique is defined as any airplane built by the original manufacturer or licensee before 1946; 'classics' are those that were built between 1946 and 1955 inclusive. [*Nigel Moll*]

BEAUTIFUL BYGONES

BELOW The Travel Air is rich in the lore of aviation. When this diminutive shape, with its distinctive elephant-ear ailerons, puttered down the taxiway under a Florida sky in 1987, aviation enthusiasts at Sun 'n Fun gazed admiringly. [*Philip Handleman*]

RIGHT The Boeing Stearman Model 75, in its many variations and corresponding designations, served as the US military's leading primary trainer during World War 2. So many thousands were built for the training effort and after the war such a large

percentage were operated as crop dusters and sprayers that today the Stearman is the most common biplane in the United States. Not surprisingly, Stearmans dominate the National Biplane Fly-In at Bartlesville, Oklahoma. Oblivious to the world only a few hundred feet below, this Stearman cruises lazily in perfect open cockpit flying weather. [*Philip Handleman*]

BELOW RIGHT It's back again, for the umpteenth time since 1929; the Great Lakes Biplane is in production in Claremont, New Hampshire. [*Nigel Moll*]

ABOVE Curtis JN-4 Jenny with a skydiver aboard. Built in 1918, the Jenny is among the oldest airplanes flying today. An example of its authenticity and frailty is the tail's touchpoint, which is a wooden skid; the World War 1 biplane therefore always operates from sod fields. When displayed on pavement, as shown here, the precious and delicate antique is pushed and pulled, not taxied, to its parking spot with the help of a two-wheel cart that elevates the tail so that the skin does not scrape along the asphalt. [*Philip Handleman*]

Top left A Travel Air beauty at the AAA Fly-In. The big wheels, overhanging ailerons, speed ring and spinner are the stuff of which flying dreams are made.

Center left An extremely rare 1946 Johnson Rocket, restored over an eight-year period by Orval Fairbairn. This postwar design boasted high performance at a reasonable price – a combination the Watsonville group would happily settle for today.

Left Many fledgling military cadets were initiated into the flying fraternity at the controls of a Ryan PT-22 Recruit. This one enlivens Watsonville.

Top Quiet and unassuming is Bob Greenhoe's 1935 Pasped Skylark, the only one ever built. Invariably, wherever he lands his special airplane with its bulbous wheel fairings and other distinctive features a crowd of curious onlookers huddles around it peppering Bob, of Alma, Michigan, with questions. Powered by a 165-hp Warner engine, the aircraft cruises at 115 mph.

Above Of course, a national biplane fly-in would not be complete without a complement of Beech Staggerwings. This one sports a protruding spinner. [*Photographs by Philip Handleman*]

LEFT The Stinson L-5 was the US Army's flying jeep in World War 2 and Korea. Its STOL capabilities and high stall/spin resistance enabled the L-5 to operate from tiny airstrips which few other types could get to in pre-helicopter days. A Marine Corps OY-1 variant was the first aircraft to land on Iwo Jima after the Americans took the island from the Japanese. [*Mike Jerram*]

BELOW Ask an American to name a light aeroplane and the chances are he will say 'Piper Cub'. Yet when some J-3 Cubs took part in the 1941 Third Army manouvers at El Paso, Texas, a sceptical cavalry brigade commander was moved to observe that they 'looked like goddammed grasshoppers out in the boondocks'. Thus the 6000 Cubs ordered by the US Army were known, like this one, as Grasshoppers, but more properly designed L-4s. Grasshoppers (readily identifiable by their extended greenhouse canopies) served in all major theaters of war up to Korea,

performing liaison and artillery spotting duties from fields, roads and launching platforms atop tank landing-craft. [*Mike Jerram*]

BELOW Huge glasshouse cabin and wide doors make the L-5 a superb camera ship. This aircraft is finished in the markings of the 13th Air Force operating out of the Philippines in World War 2. [*Mike Jerram*]

BOTTOM Walter Beech's Model 17 biplane, colloqually known as the Staggerwing because of its unusual negative-stagger wing arrangement, was as fast as the latest US military pursuit aircraft when the first models appeared in 1932, and is one of the most sought after antiques, with 200 mph cruise speed and a roomy cabin seating five. This 450-hp Pratt & Whitney Wasp-powered Beechcraft has been restored by Staggerwing buff Glenn McNabb of Jasper, Tennessee in the Navy colors it wore during wartime service as a GB-2. [*Mike Jerram*]

BEAUTIFUL BYGONES

Another sparkling Beech Staggerwing at the 1987 Sun 'n Fun in Florida. Ahead of its time, the Stag featured an aerodynamic teardrop shape, an enclosed cabin, retractable landing gear and 'I'-shaped wing struts. The wings have an unusual negative stagger, which means the lower wing's leading edge extends forward of the upper wing's leading edge. It was an uncommonly fast airplane for the late 1930s, even able to outrun many military types of the period. In wartime Staggerwings were used by the USAAF, US Navy and British Fleet Air Arm for communications duties and VIP transport. [*Philip Handleman*]

BEAUTIFUL BYGONES

BELOW This immaculately restored Stag occupies a special place at Sun 'n Fun. [*Philip Handleman*]

BOTTOM Joining the company of Staggerwings in the tie-down circle for special restorations at Sun 'n Fun is this stunning Stinson Reliant. Often called the gullwing Stinson, for obvious reasons, this type was a sturdy workhorse in an earlier era. This gullwing Stinson has a bumped cowl, rarely seen these days. A special touch is the duplication of the fuselage trim stripe on the wheel fairings. [*Philip Handleman*]

RIGHT Ken Flaglor's Gee Bee Y, built in 1984 but based on a 1930s design, has a 300-hp Lycoming R-680-13. Hanging from nearly all the display airplanes at Oshkosh is a specifications card giving the leading data. Like many homebuilders, Flaglor left blank the line for 'Cost to build'. [*Nigel Moll*]

BELOW RIGHT The Bartlesville biplane gathering sees an amazing assemblage of brilliant restorations, like this red Stearman. [*Philip Handleman*]

BEAUTIFUL BYGONES

Antiques and classics line-up at Oshkosh in 1984 shows the many configurations of the 'golden oldies' era. For one week each year the tranquil Wisconsin town is transformed by an influx of over 800,000 aviation enthusiasts. [*Nigel Moll*]

BELOW This replica of Charles Lindbergh's *Spirit of St. Louis* was built by the EAA Foundation and flown on a national tour of 107 cities in 48 states to commemorate the 50th anniversary of Lindbergh's achievement. Lindbergh took off in the 220-hp Ryan monoplane on 20 May 1927 from Roosevelt Field, Long Island, New York and landed at Le Bourget airfield, Paris, having flown 3610 miles. The prize for the first solo transatlantic flight was $25,000. [*Nigel Moll*]

RIGHT A Ryan monoplane, similar to the beloved PT-22 Recruit, taxies to take-off position during the World War 2 light trainer fly-bys at Madera. Note the lone cockpit, speed ring and wheel fairings. [*Philip Handleman*]

BELOW RIGHT A close-up of a Ryan PT-22, the 'PT' standing for the airplane's role when it was in military service – that of primary trainer. [*Nigel Moll*]

BELOW The sparkling 1950 Trojan belonging to Nancy Grout, profiled at Oshkosh in 1984. Some of the relics that appear there each year have been flying all their lives, but that's by no means always the case. Many have been rescued from ruin by enthusiasts who spotted their wingless or engineless carcases rotting in the long grass of quiet rural airfields. Others are found hanging from the rafters of barns, abandoned and forgotten decades ago. No matter how extensive the delapidation, as long as the manufacturer's plate is still attached, that's all that is required for the restoration to begin. Sometimes a 'restored' antique is actually virtually brand new, the majority of its components having been handbuilt from scratch with reference to the original plans – if they exist. Thousands of dollars and hours can go into an extensive rebuild. [*Nigel Moll*]

TRAINER TRIBUTES

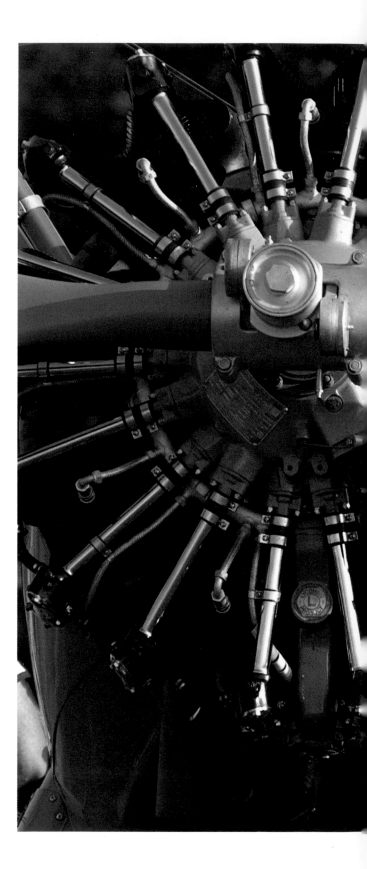

Many Oshkosh visitors had their first taste of flying in airplanes like these Stearmans, with the bellow of a big radial, its cylinders out in the breeze. Paradoxically Lloyd Stearman played no part in the design of the classic American biplane which bears his name; he left the Wichita company in 1932, two years before designers Harold Zipp and Jack Clark unveiled their first Stearman Model 70 from which the Army PT-13/17 and Navy N2Ss evolved. [*Nigel Moll*]

ABOVE Two Navy Stearmans in formation pass low over the airport at Bartlesville during the annual National Antique Airplane Association Fly-In, 1987. The lush green hills in the background nicely silhouette the Stearmans. For many years the AAA held its annual fly-in at its headquarters – Antique Airfield near Blakesburg, Iowa – but because of the short grass runways there, some would-be participants did not come. The decision was made to rectify this inadequacy by changing the venue of the annual fly-in to an airport able to accommodate all antique airplanes. The ultimate choice was Bartlesville, Oklahoma with its 6200-foot long runway. The airport had been used earlier in the year by the National Biplane Association for its first National fly-in. The Bartlesville Chamber of Commerce displayed special interest in attracting additional visitors to the local area during the petroleum industry's doldrums – the town is the home of Phillips. [*Philip Handleman*]

ABOVE LEFT The Stearman training biplane was one of the few things the US Army and Navy ever agreed upon: both services ordered the aircraft in the mid-1930s, using it as a primary trainer throughout World War 2, and altogether some 10,346 were built. This handsome specimen is restored as a Navy N2S-5, powered by a 225-hp Lycoming R680 engine. [*Mike Jerram*]

LEFT This immaculate Stearman, the proud mount of Harry Thomas, stands out even among the many sparkling restorations at the 1987 Galesburg Stearman Fly-In. Fitted with a 300 Lycoming engine she sports a full cowl, polished spinner, wheel fairings and a headrest. The blue trim nicely accents the shiny yellow of this award winner. [*Philip Handleman*]

ABOVE All teeth, but not much bite. The Fairchild PT-26 was strictly a non-combatant World War 2 primary trainer, powered by a 200-hp Ranger L-440-3 in-line engine. The aircraft evolved from the similar, but lower powered PT-19 of 1940, and was used by the US Army Air Corps and Royal Canadian Air Force, who called theirs the Cornell. [*Mike Jerram*]

ABOVE RIGHT Often mistaken for a Stearman, this is an N3N, conceived and constructed by the US Navy as a primary trainer. The N3N, along with the Stearman, was known in the Navy as the Yellow Peril. Among the features that distinguish it from the Stearman are the aileron connector struts aft of the 'N' struts between the wing. [*Philip Handleman*]

RIGHT A contemporary of the Stearman, the Naval Aircraft factory N3N was manufactured by the US Navy's own plant at the Philadelphia Navy Yard. It was unusual in having a bolted steel tube fuselage with removable metal panels for ease of maintenance access. The N3Ns served in primary training schools throughout World War 2 and a few, equipped with floats, were retained by the US Naval Academy for training midshipmen as late as 1961 – the last biplanes to see military service following the USAF's disposal of its Stearmans in 1948. This aircraft is an N3N-3, powered by a 235-hp Wright R-760-2 radial engine. [*Mike Jerram*]

TRAINER TRIBUTES

BELOW *Pop-pop-pop* goes the Kinner on the Ryan P-22 Recruit, forever sounding as if it's only running on four of its five cylinders. [*Mike Jerram*]

BOTTOM US army flight cadets graduated from PT-17 Stearmans or Fairchild PT-19/26s onto the consolidated Vultee BT-13 before they were let loose on AT-6s. Officially known as the valiant, any BT-13 trained pilot will tell you the aeroplane's real name: *Vibrator*, because the 450-hp Pratt & Whitney Wasp-engined trainer was noted for the all-over massage job it provided in flight. More than 11,000 were built, but few survive in flying condition. [*Mike Jerram*]

RIGHT This rare Timm N2T-1 Tutor featured a patented form of plastic-bonded plywood construction called Aeromold which resulted in a very smooth, drag-free surface giving more performance per horsepower than contemporary wood or fabric-skinned trainers. [*Mike Jerram*]

CENTER RIGHT Only occasionally seen is the metal-fuselaged Meyers OTW. Not too many were built, but those that do appear on the airshow circuit are almost always in good shape—perhaps reflecting their non-use as dusters and sprayers. [*Philip Handleman*]

BOTTOM RIGHT During the course of the American airshow season it's possible to come across a few examples of this beautiful rare biplane, refered to affectionately by old-timers as the Bird plane. Its distinguishing feature is the enormous camber and span of the upper wing in relation to its meager sized lower wing. [*Philip Handleman*]

ABOVE Neat cowl job on the 160 hp Kinner radial engine and 'elbow' jointed undercarriage legs characterize the Ryan PT-22 Recruit primary trainer which joined the US Army Air Corps; 1023 were built for the Army and Navy. The aircraft was developed from the civilian ST series of two-seat trainers and aerobatic aircraft which had Menasco in-line engines. The PT-22 had swept-back wings (a modest four degrees) roomier cockpits to accommodate pilots in full military flight gear, and lacked the undercarriage 'trouser' fairings of the civilian variantes. Despite the external wire bracing the PT-22 was among the fastest primary trainers, cruising around 120 mph, and is renowned for its sprightly snap-rolls – not always entirely voluntary on the part of its pilots. [*Mike Jerram*]

ABOVE LEFT Amid rows of beautifully restored aircraft at the AAA Fly-In rests a Ryan PT-22 Recruit. This airplane has been restored with some authenticity for its metal fuselage has been left bare while its wings and control surfaces have been painted high-visibility yellow. [*Philip Handleman*]

LEFT The US Army Air Corps took delivery of the Recruit, its first low-wing monoplane trainer, in 1939. The Aircraft was the shape of wings to come for the USAAC, and was derived from a series of Ryan trainers which began with the ST Sport in 1934. In many ways it was advanced for its time, with disc brakes and a steerable tailwheel. [*Norman Pealing*]

BELOW 'He was coming at me like this, see' . . . a group of veteran T-6ers gather round *Ms. Hazel* to relive magic moments at Harlingen. The T-6 has a maximum speed of 206 mph, cruises at 180 mph at 11,000 feet and lands at 66 mph – fast in the immediate post-biplane era. [*Norman Pealing*]

BELOW To the Army they were T-6s; the Navy called theirs SNJs; Brits and Canucks prefered Harvard. Whichever, North American's trainer was an exciting prospect for trainee pilots: 550 hp, retractable undercarriage, not too difficult to imagine yourself in one of the fighters on the recruiting posters. Rookie pilots training under the Commonwealth Air Training Plan moved up to Harvards after 65 hours flying on Tiger Moth or Fleet Finch biplanes. The USAAC used their AT-6s for advanced training, but eventually dispensed with the 'A' designation and used the aircraft for basic instruction, putting new recruits straight into the T-6's big cockpit. AT-6s/SNJ-5s are popular now for the same reasons they were liked in the military: they were and still are trainers. Today they prepare pilots for more potent warbirds, such as P-51 Mustangs, just as they did in the 1940s. 'Tee-Six Time' is a prerequisite of being let loose in the rarer machinery, although many a P-51 pilot says the old trainer is more demanding to fly than the fancy ones. Not all AT-6 owners, however, have their eye on the more exotic warbirds; most are happy to fly the T-6 for its own sake, rather than for what it could be preparing them to fly. It's a demanding airplane, and thus a satisfying one. This bright yellow Harvard in Royal Canadian Air Force colors is owned by Len Fallowfield of Ontario. [*Mike Jerram*]

BELOW Where better for Texans to roost than Rebel Field, Texas? The Confederate Air Force show is a magnet for T-6 owners and 'Colonels' across the nation. No less than 50,000 USAAF pilots, plus another 40,000 from the Navy, learned to fly on this trainer to end trainers. [*Norman Pealing*]

BELOW Good forward vision was not a T-6 strongpoint, so trainees had to remember to weave from side to side while taxiing, rudders waggling like ducks' tails. More than a few inadvertently sawed the tail off the T-6 ahead. The prototype began as the NA-16, which first flew in April 1935 and was powered by a 400-hp Wright R-975 Whirlwind radial; most T-6s have Pratt & Whitney engines of 550 hp. The Texan entered production in 1938 and remained the USAF's basic and advanced trainer until 1956. NAA had built 15,109 T-6s by 1945, and versions were built in Australia as the Wirraway, by Noorduyn in Canada, in Japan (earning the Allied codename *Oak*) and by Saab in Sweden. Canadian Car & Foundry also built 555 T-6Gs in 1951–54 for FAC (forward air control) work in Korea. Altogether the air arm of 34 foreign nations were helped to qualify by the T-6, and surplus T-6s have appeared in large numbers in recent years as the smaller European air forces finally replace them with modern trainers. [*Mike Jerram*]

ABOVE This Navy SNJ-5 (note the arrestor hook) belongs to Warbirds of American director Jerry Walbrun, who regularly leads airshow formations of up to 32 T-6s/SNJs/Harvards. The buzz-saw rasp of all those Wasp engines and the howl of near-supersonic propeller tips which characterize the aircraft is pure heaven for some, sheer masochism for anti-noise campaigners. [*Mike Jerram*]

ABOVE LEFT Tight formation take-off by a pair of T-6s at the EAA Convention at Oshkosh. The aircraft nearest the camera is a remanufactured T-6G, some 700 of which were updated from earlier marks in 1950 with new clear-vision canopies, increased fuel tankage and upgraded instrumentation. Some were used during the Korean War as forward air control spotters, directing air strikes against North Korean positions. [*Mike Jerram*]

LEFT A great many Texans were left in natural metal finish, like this ex-Royal Canadian Air force example. Although usually unarmed, the T-6 could be fitted with a 0.30 or .303 caliber machine-gun in the right outer wing panel for gunnery practise. Trainee gunners learned how to shoot from the rear cockpit of an AT-6 or SNJ, the rear section of the canopy folding up and over. [*Norman Pealing*]

ABOVE RIGHT Military color schemes are not essential for T-6s, but few owners can resist the temptation to give their birds a warlike appearance. This British-owned example is in USAAF markings. [*Mike Jerram*]

RIGHT Californians Dennis Buehn and Randy Difani used a Canadian Harvard airframe to recreate this North American BC-2 basic combat trainer prototype of 1939. Major surgery included the installation of a geared Pratt & Whitney R-1340 engine driving a three-bladed propeller, extended cowling, control surface gap seals, new rudder, wing incidence reduction and an extensive weight reduction program. [*Mike Jerram*]

TRAINER TRIBUTES

BELOW The North American T-28 was the T-6's successor, serving with the USAF, US Navy and Marine Corps as a basic and instrument trainer from 1950 onwards. Power comes from an 800-hp Wright R-1300 seven-cylinder radial engine. This T-28B is finished in the blue and gold colors of the US Navy's

Blue Angels flight demonstration team – for reasons best known to owner J. M. Ellis III, since the Blues never operated the aircraft. [*Mike Jerram*]

RIGHT, TOP Bob Urbine's yellow bird is an ex-USAF T-28A upgraded to T-28D standard. [*Mike Jerram*]

Bottom The US Navy ordered 489 T-28Bs in 1952 and three years later came back for another 299 T-28Cs which had strengthened landing gear, smaller diameter propellers and arrestor hooks for operations from training carriers for pilot deck landing qualification. This restored example wears the yellow training colors of Navy squadron VT-2 which operated T-28Bs from NAS Whiting Field until the late 1970s, when they were replaced by Beech T-34C Turbo Mentors. However, the large diameter nosewheel and high-profile canopy suggests that the aircraft is an impostor, probably an ex-USAF T-28A/D. [*Mike Jerram*]

LEFT T-28s were widely exported to overseas customers including the South Vietnamese Air Force–whose colors are worn by this T-28D. [*Mike Jerram*]

BELOW Dave Schwartz's T-28 is a C model, formerly a US Navy trainer restored in the colors of the South

Vietnamese Air Force's 1st Air Commando unit. Gun-pods, rockets, 500 lb bombs and napalm were carried by VNAF T-28s between 1963–65. [*Mike Jerram*]

BOTTOM Despite its barrel-chested look, the T-28 is one of the nicest flying warbirds. [*Nigel Moll*]

ABOVE Like the Harvard, the Beech T-34 makes a splendid formation aircraft. Here three select smoke as they fly by over Harlingen. [*Norman Pealing*]

LEFT This highly buffed T-34A bears the colors of the Special Air Missions wing of the USAF, which transports VIPs including incumbents of the White House – though Presidents and First Ladies do not travel in single-engine trainers. [*Mike Jerram*]

RIGHT An immaculate T-34 pictured at Oshkosh in 1984. [*Nigel Moll*]

BELOW This close-up shows just how roomy the T-34's cockpit is: flying Mike Brady's Mentor is his assistant chief pilot, Jim Gardner. This aircraft has full dual controls, is fully aerobatic and boasts a host of hi-tech avionics, including color weather radar. Michael J. Brady is the founder and 'boss' of Northwest Airlink, a leading regional carrier in the US, and he likes to relax by flying his beautifully restored Beech Mentor. He bought the T-34 from Fred Smith (the main man at FedEx), since when he has lavished many hours of loving care on the aircraft. Mike's attention to detail was rewarded at Oshkosh in 1987 when his aircraft earned a prize in a competition which he didn't mean to enter! The T-34 is powered by a 225-hp Continental O-470-13A 'flat-six' engine, giving a maximum speed of 189 mph at sea level. Some Mentors had 340-hp Lycomings. [*Norman Pealing*]

RIGHT Mike Brady turns final in his T-34 – note the Bonanza-type landing gear. The Mentor weighs in at just over 3300 lb at take-off and has a service ceiling of 26,800 feet. Visibility for both student and instructor is excellent – and with a range of 600 miles, there's plenty of endurance for a worthwhile training session. [*Norman Pealing*]

BELOW RIGHT The Bonanza's influence on the design is apparent in this view of the T-34. Beech developed the Mentor as a private venture and the trainer made its maiden flight on 2 December 1948. After being evaluated as the YT-34 in 1950, the USAF placed an order for 350 T-34As, followed by 423 T-34Bs for the Navy. The B45 export model was ordered by Argentina, Chile, Colombia, Mexico, El Salvador and Venezuela. Canadian Car & Foundry also built 56, of which 24 were supplied to Turkey, and Fuji manufactured 126 under license for the Japanese Self-Defense force. [*Norman Pealing*]

LEFT Successful winner of a contest to find a replacement for the North American T-6 in the USAF inventory, Beechcraft's T-34 Mentor served as a basic trainer with the USAF and US Navy, and was manufactured under license in Japan by Fuji Industries. The example pictured here is a Wichita-built Mentor, restored to Japanese Self-Defense Force colors. [*Mike Jerram*]

RIGHT The US Navy received 423 Beech T-34B Mentor primary trainers between 1954–57: this one is a privately owned aircraft in 1950s chrome yellow Navy trainer colors. Few piston-engined Mentors remain in service with the US Navy, having been superseded by the Pratt & Whitney PT-6 turbine-engined T-34C Turbo Mentor. [*Mike Jerram*]

BELOW A pair of T-34s take off to formate for another mass flypast at Oshkosh in 1984. [*Nigel Moll*]

PORTRAITS OF POWER

Hot and heavy – throttles full forward! At the 24th Reno Air Races in 1987, Lefty Gardner is at the controls of his distinctive P-38 *White Lit'nin*, Skip Holm is piloting Joe Kasparoff's P-51 *The Healer*. Reno is synonymous with speed. Each year the racing pilots assemble in Nevada for a series of heats in different aircraft categories to see who is the fastest, and with a few exceptions the most exciting categories consist of World War 2 era aircraft. In many cases these former warplanes have been substantially modified to eke out every last ounce of horsepower. While the basic airframes date from an earlier generation, the ongoing improvements usually result in slightly enhanced performance statistics for the piston-powered muscle machines in each succeeding year of the Reno races. [*Philip Handleman*]

LEFT Lefty Gardner's P-38 is part racer, part airshow mount. His racing is characterized by his ability to get the Lightning's wingtip closer to the desert than anyone else dares, while his aerobatic routine includes some spectacular engine-out work including low-level rolls into the dead engine – a technique once thought to be a certain way to 'buy the farm'. [*Mike Jerram*]

RIGHT Lefty's P-38 is the only Unlimited racer at Reno which *intentionally* streams smoke from its engines: he has an effective smoke-generating system with which he traces his aerobatic figures. [*Mike Jerram*]

BELOW Former cropduster and one of the founders of the Confederate Air Force, Lefty Gardner is a Reno regular in his #13 *White Lit'nin*, which he races and flies in the daily airshows. [*Nigel Moll*]

LEFT Though uncompetitive with the best Unlimiteds, the fork-tailed devil gets lower than anything else as Lefty Gardner dusts the desert. His racing around the pylons is consistently among the most spectacular of the flying—although, with its superchargers removed, the airplane is not particularly fast. [*Philip Handleman*]

RIGHT Lefty Gardner and P-38 #13 in full fury in 1982. It qualified at 345.376 mph and flew into third place in the Bronze final at 335.201 mph. He seems to have a peculiarly accurate feel for his wingspan, and places the tip low, very low, in turns. [*Nigel Moll*]

BELOW The sleek twin-boom design of the Lightning is evident as Lefty whisks past the famous Reno finishing pylon in 1987. [*Philip Handleman*]

PORTRAITS OF POWER

Wiley Sanders's #69 *Jeannie*, formerly *Galloping Ghost* and *Miss Candace*, took Gold at Reno in successive years – 1980 in the hands of Mac McClain at 433.01 mph, and in 1981 with Skip Holm at 431.29 mph after qualifying at a record 450.09 mph. Looking for a hat-trick in 1982, she threw a con-rod during pre-qualifying practise. But after a 15-hour engine change – with the help and floodlights of a competing crew (Tired Iron of P-51 #81 *Habu*) – that extended well past midnight, *Jeannie* was again in with a chance. Until, that is, she blew a second engine while trying to qualify the next day. The prop

governor let go and *Jeannie* howled like a hyena as pilot Skip Holm pulled up to trade speed for altitude. Reno old-timers feared the prop would throw a blade, so loud was the wail; but Holm, despite an oil-covered windshield, made a superb deadstick touchdown that kept *Jeannie* free of further damage. The pits erupted in a cheer for his performance, but the plane was not to race at Reno 82. *Jeannie* now performs as the *Leeward Air Ranch Special*. [*Nigel Moll*]

ABOVE AND LEFT *Specter* and #44 *Leeward Air Ranch Special*, seen here in 1983 and 1984, are one and the same aircraft. It has the longest pedigree and most colorful history in Unlimited racing. [*Philip Wallick*]

ABOVE RIGHT AND RIGHT The plane's achievements are recounted on the engraved landing gear leg cover of the repainted #9. As #77 *Galloping Ghost* the then stock Mustang took part in the postwar Thompson, Sohio and Tinnerman Trophy races at Cleveland. She did not race during most of the 1960s but emerged at the revived Reno National Air Races as Cliff Cummins' radically modified #69 *Miss Candace*, flying and racing under that name until 1979. *Jeannie* was then renamed after the wife of the new owner, Wiley Sanders. [*Philip Wallick*]

PORTRAITS OF POWER

BELOW AND RIGHT At Reno 88 Jimmy Leeward, a property developer from Ocala, Florida, qualified the *Leeward Air Ranch Special* fourth fastest at 457.078 mph, but during Gold group Heat 3A on Saturday he called a 'Mayday'. Finding an unauthorized fuel truck blocking the emergency runway, Leeward set his Mustang down on a dirt road, bounced into the sagebrush and damaged his propeller. [*Philip Wallick*]

BELOW RIGHT Plagued throughout the Reno week, *Leeward* finally pulled out with a broken cylinder during Saturday's Heat 3B. 'Maybe next year,' he consoled himself. [*Philip Wallick*]

LEFT *Dago Red* made history at Reno 82 by winning on its first outing. The airplane flew only three weeks before race week, making its victory all the more impressive. Owners Frank Taylor and Bill 'Tiger' Destefani spent, between them, about $500,000 to get *Dago Red* ready for racing. According to pilot Ron Hevle, the plan was to blow one engine in qualifying and set a new record, and then to race with a second engine. But there wasn't time. Hevle kept *Dago Red*'s race boost and reduction-gear ratio a secret, but one pit crew member foresaw the engine turning at up to 4000 rpm. He also revealed some of the measures that would help boost power to almost double the normal 1800 hp for take-off and 1600 maximum continuous. The *Dago Red* team, according to this pit crew member, had access to 18 Rolls-Royce Griffons – and intended to break the *Red Baron* Griffon Mustang's 499.018 mph record by some 30 mph. [*Nigel Moll*]

RIGHT *Dago Red* in full, furious flight round pylon 7 in the 1982 Unlimited Gold final, with victory just seconds away. [*Nigel Moll*]

BELOW An exuberant crew rides *Dago Red* back to the pits. For Hevle, Destefani, Taylor and the entire *Dago Red* team, Reno 82 was a dream come true. At Reno 81, the airplane was little more than an idea, but one year later it was the Unlimited champion at its first races. [*Nigel Moll*]

RIGHT AND FAR RIGHT Apart from the satisfaction of victory, Bakersfield cropduster Ron Hevle received the coveted trophy and a check for $26,608. His winning speed in the Gold final, 405.092, would have been higher if John Crocker in #6 *Sumthin' Else* had continued to hound him around the pylons, but after Crocker dropped out with a blown engine Hevle throttled back and loafed across the finish line. There was simply no point in taking the Merlin to its limits when the race was virtually in the bag. [*Nigel Moll*]

PORTRAITS OF POWER

BELOW Bill 'Tiger' Destefani and Frank Taylor built up the beautiful #4 *Dago Red* in less than a year for Reno 82, the first time that an all-new racer had ever swept the board first time out. [*Nigel Moll*]

RIGHT On 30 July 1983 Frank Taylor flew *Dago Red* over a 15/25 kilometre course at Mojave to set a

piston-engined world speed record of 517.06 mph. [*Philip Wallick*]

BELOW RIGHT Rick Brickert had to call a 'Mayday' after *Dago Red's* Rolls-Royce/Packard V-1650-9 threw a conrod and caught fire during the 1984 Gold final. [*Philip Wallick*]

LEFT *Dago Red*'s pilot Rick Brickert explains his tactics after clocking 412.122 mph in Unlimited Heat 3A in 1985. Brickert placed third in the Gold final, completing the eight-lap race at an average 426.848 mph. [*Mike Jerram*]

BELOW, RIGHT AND FAR RIGHT The 1982 champion was back at Reno 85, recovered from the fire which forced it out of the Unlimited Gold event in '84. Few Unlimited owners talk money, but *Dago*'s master Frank Taylor allowed that the P-51's development at that point left little change out of half a million dollars. [*Mike Jerram*]

PORTRAITS OF POWER

Rick Brickert brings Frank Taylor's P-51D *Dago Red*
home in 1985 after running fourth in Heat 2A. *Dago*,
given its head, added nearly 40 mph to its heat speed
in the Gold final, placing third at 426.848 mph.
[*Mike Jerram*]

BELOW LEFT, BELOW AND RIGHT Dallas real estate developer Alan Preston is the current owner of *Dago Red*. In 1986 Preston became the first pilot to take part in all four Reno classes – Unlimited, T-6, International Formula Midget and Biplane – and took Gold in IFM and Biplane in 1988. At rest Dago's cockpit looks cosy enough, but going around the course at speed Preston says 'it's like being in a 450-mph washing-machine. It's noisy, it's loud, it vibrates . . .' Preston is a hard charger, but the Unlimited Championship has so far eluded him. 'Coming second is like kissing your sister,' he says ruefully. [*Photographs by Philip Wallick*]

PORTRAITS OF POWER

BELOW Ken Burnstine brought *Foxy Lady* to Reno in 1974, fresh from a rebuild from stock P-51D configuration by Leroy Penhall's Fighter Imports at Chino, California. The sleek Mustang arrived in a sinister all-black color scheme and had its attractive decoration added by hand in the pit area. To no avail, sadly. Engine problems prevented *Foxy Lady* from qualifying, but for consolation Burnstine took his stock P-51 *Miss Suzi Q* to victory in the Gold. After Burnstine's death at Mojave in 1975 John Crocker

bought *Foxy Lady* and she became the 1979 Gold Champion *Sumthin' Else*. [*Philip Wallick*]

BOTTOM Crocker's luck ran out in the 1982 Unlimited Gold final when *Sumthin' Else* pulled out after three good laps. The Merlin was turning at 3750 rpm and ran out of induction cooling. With the induction temperature at 100° the engine detonated once, snapping the crankshaft in half. The engine then tore its own innards apart. With oil covering the cowling

and windshield, Crocker made a blind landing under the guidance of pace pilot Bob Hoover circling overhead in the yellow Rockwell International P-51. When running on 145-octane avgas, the engine turns out somewhere between 3200 and 3400 hp, according to Crocker. The most powerful Merlins at Reno turn out almost double their military horsepower, so some mechanical failures are inevitable. [*Nigel Moll*]

BELOW DC-10 check captain John Crocker was again a target for the Reno gremlins in 1985. With his slick Mustang #6 *Sumthin' Else* running well up with the leaders in Saturday's Heat 3A, the P-51D's Merlin backfired, causing serious damage and threatening Crocker's place in the Gold final. *Sumthin' Else* was back on the start line come Sunday, only to pull out on lap five with a blown engine. [*Mike Jerram*]

BOTTOM Crocker warms up his Merlin at Reno in 1988. [*Philip Wallick*]

PORTRAITS OF POWER

Since his first rookie race in 1973 World Airlines captain John Crocker has been a popular and competitive racer at Reno. On his first appearance with #6 *Sumthin' Else* in 1976 he was one of three pilots to break the qualifying speed record on three successive days and became National Air Race Champion in the eventful Gold final of 1979, which he won at 422.30 mph. At Reno 88 *Sumthin' Else* appeared in this attractive color scheme, but was relegated to second place in the 'Super Stocks' Silver final after Crocker incurred a 16-second penalty for cutting pylon 1 on lap 4. [*Philip Wallick*]

BELOW On 14 August 1979 Steve Hinton and the *Red Baron* broke Greenamyer's world speed record for piston-engined aircraft, streaking across a three-kilometre course at Tonopah, Nevada at 499.018 mph. Three weeks later Hinton, his Griffon engine sounding sick, trailed John Crocker's P-51 *Sumthin' Else* across the Gold final finish line, pulled up and began a turn for an emergency landing on Stead Airport's Runway 26. He never made it. The *Baron*'s engine seized, all six propblades went to flat pitch, acting like an enormous airbrake, and the beautiful RB-51 slammed into the Lemon Valley. Bob Hoover,

circling above, believed that no one could have survived the wreck, but Steve was found alive, with multiple injuries, still in his seat. [*Philip Wallick*]

BOTTOM *Red Baron* in its original Merlin-engined form when flown by Mac McClain at Reno 74, prior to its transformation into the RB-51. [*Philip Wallick*]

CENTER Blown engine? Never fear, Mike is here. Mike Wilton brought this Packard-built V-1650-9A in the back of a Chevy van in 1982 – just in case. The price was $40,000 'this week only'. This particular

Merlin powered *Red Baron* before being replaced by a Rolls-Royce Griffon. [*Nigel Moll*]

BELOW P-51 #5 had a long history of Reno racing, having previously been Chuck Hall's *Miss R J* and Gunther Balz's 1972 Gold-winning *Roto-Finish Special*. Acquired by Ed Browning of Red Baron Flying Services in Idaho Falls in the early 1970s, it underwent the most extensive Mustang transformation then undertaken. Browning, assisted by airframe gurus Bruce Boland and Pete Law and engine wizards Dave Zeuschel and Randy Scoville,

replaced its Merlin engine with a Rolls-Royce Griffon 74 from a British Avro Shackleton maritime patrol aircraft, driving contra-rotating props, and made such fundamental changes to the airframe that the new designation RB-51 was considered appropriate. After making its Reno debut in 1975 it took two years to get *Red Baron* truly sorted, before Reno's 'winningest' pilot Darryl Greenamyer swept the field in 1977 to take his seventh Gold victory at a new race record speed of 430.70 mph. The following year Steve Hinton became the *Baron's* pilot and took the RB-51 to its second Reno victory. [*Philip Wallick*]

The Whittington brothers from Fort Lauderdale,
Florida spent five years putting together #09 *Precious
Metal*. [*Philip Wallick*]

LEFT Don Whittington latches *Precious Metal*'s canopy in preparation for the Gold final in 1988. It would be a dramatic trip. [*Philip Wallick*]

BELOW Despite the name *Precious Metal* shares only the tail cone of the brothers' previous Mustang, most of this aircraft being brand new. [*Philip Wallick*]

BELOW Like *Red Baron*, *Precious Metal* is powered by a Rolls-Royce Griffon engine driving contra-rotating propellers—and is arguably the most attractive racing conversion of a Mustang yet. [*Philip Wallick*]

BOTTOM Down and out. Like the defending champion *Red Baron* nine years previously the Griffon-engined Mustang ended up in the dirt of Reno's Lemon Valley, though Don Whittington successfully bellied *Precious Metal* onto the dry lake bed—and vowed to have it flying again before year's end. [*Philip Wallick*]

'Just as Bob Hoover called "Gentlemen, you have a race," I pushed it up a little more' recalled *Precious Metal* pilot Don Whittington. 'I was adding power, and just at that point Hoover had already pulled up and we were coming up on the Interstate. That's when it happened. The propeller governor failed and the blades went the other direction – the rpms went to 5500 or 6000 and blew the spinner apart. My first thought was that I was going to have to get out because it was shaking rather badly. I started to do

that, but that wouldn't work because I realized that I was going too slow. I had already slowed down to roughly 130 indicated. I looked down and could see I was over a populated area, so I pushed everything back up, and it didn't shake any worse. I went ahead and turned the mag switch back on and it fired. I gave it a little throttle to get a little airspeed going forward, because it was coming down, and I mean it was coming *straight* down!' Fortunately Whittington walked away from the disaster. [*Philip Wallick*]

Above left Bill 'Tiger' Destefani returned to Reno in 1983 with yet another brand-new and radically modified Mustang, #7 *Strega* – Italian for 'witch'. [*Philip Wallick*]

Left After five years of disappointment the witch finally cast her spell for the *Strega* team in 1987 when Bill Destefani beat 1986 winner Rick Brickert in *Dreadnought* to set a new Gold race speed record of 452.559 mph. The battle is pictured on page 166. However, oil starvation resulted in a blown Merlin during a qualifying round in 1988. [*Philip Wallick*]

Above *Strega* was on its third Reno outing in 1985. A cracked blower during the warm up for the start of Heat 2A brought pilot Ron Hevle back to the runway and meant a long night for the pit crew. Next day a carburettor problem again prematurely aborted Hevle's heat race on lap 6. The run of misfortune continued into the Gold final, when a film of oil on the windscreen signaled a broken piston and Hevle dropped back from the pre-race formation before it climbed over the mountains for the run-in to the start. [*Mike Jerram*]

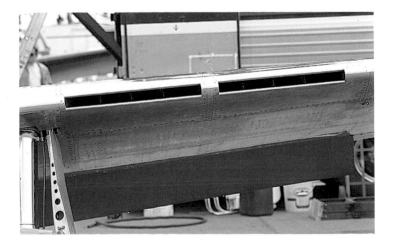

ABOVE AND LEFT Alan Preston's #84 *Stiletto*, which suitably won the 1984 Unlimited Championship at 437.62 mph, is thus far the most-modified P-51D to race at Reno. The characteristic ventral cooling scoop has been deleted and replaced by flush inlets in the wing leading edges and computer-controled cooling spraybars, the wing area savagely reduced to slightly less than that of a 100 hp Cessna 150 trainer. Engine and mechanical problems dogged Skip Holm's 1985 challenge, and a balky landing gear leg finally destroyed *Stiletto*'s chances of pulling off consecutive wins. [*Mike Jerram*]

ABOVE LEFT *Stiletto* was favored by many to achieve its second consecutive Reno victory in 1985. Despite a thrown rod and an engine change during qualification, the heavily modified Mustang was on the start line for Sunday's Gold final, but after take-off the right gear leg refused to retract and although pilot Skip Holm's indulged in some aerobatic, G-pulling efforts to stow the gear, he was unable to get *Stiletto* cleaned up in time for the airborne start and had to retire. [*Mike Jerram*]

ABOVE Jimmie McMillan's Douglas AD-4N Skyraider really did lead Skip Holm's slippery *Stiletto* in 1985, but only for this brief moment during the Unlimited qualifying runs. The lumbering Spad did make it through to the finish of racing, however, gaining seventh place in the Bronze division. [*Mike Jerram*]

LEFT, RIGHT AND FAR RIGHT A rattlesnake's-eye view of race preparations for Scott Sherman's #84 *Stiletto*. The plane was developed by Alan Preston, now owner of *Dago Red*, and is quite different in concept from other 'Super Mustangs'. Skip Holm, an Edwards Air Force Base-trained test pilot, flew *Stiletto* to victory in the 1984 Gold event at 437.62 mph. 'I like flying Mustangs, and my favorite would have to be *Stiletto*,' he says. 'She was honed to be the closest to what you would want in a racing Mustang. *Jeannie* is a great airplane... but *Stiletto* took the refinement a step further and took care of some of the problems with *Jeannie*, but we also probably made the airplane more difficult to maintain and fly.' New owner/pilot Scott Sherman, who runs an aircraft sales company in North Palm Beach, Florida reports: 'It's a bit like flying a jet. It's a real nice flying machine, but when you're running at high power you know that you're sitting behind that hand grenade. You're just playing the odds.' The odds were against him in 1988: Sherman 'Maydayed' out of the Gold final. [*Philip Wallick*]

RIGHT Framed against the Reno landscape, the muscular looking P-51 *Stiletto* is always a formidable contender in the Unlimited class. [*Philip Wallick*]

BELOW Something borrowed... *Stiletto* briefly wore *Dago Red*'s rudder at the 1986 races, but failed to finish in the Gold event, while the donor placed fourth. [*Philip Wallick*]

LEFT AND BELOW LEFT Texas cropduster and Confederate Air Force founder member Lefty Gardner puts his working skills to good effect rounding the Reno pylons in his P-51D *Thunderbird* (and his P-38 *White Lit'nin* – see pages 76–81): lower than the competition. 'I'm real comfortable flying low to the ground . . . when you get cranked up and going fast, you get on your toes and really become alert, all your faculties are there.' Is it true that Lefty once taxied back to the pits with sagebrush on his wingtip? 'It's true. I did hit a sagebrush in 1980, but it wasn't

that short. The bush was at least 10 or 12 feet tall!' Lefty and *Thunderbird* were National Champions in 1976 at 379.61 mph. [*Philip Wallick*]

BELOW The 63-year-old veteran Lefty Gardner had two cracks at the Unlimited races in 1985 with *White Lit'nin* and *Thunderbird*, the latter seen here rounding pylon 6 during Saturday's Heat 3B, which he won at 377.321 mph. The USAF Thunderbirds never actually flew P-51Ds, but who would argue with such a gorgeous color scheme? [*Mike Jerram*]

Above Is it a Learjet? Is it a Mustang? Actually, it's a bit of both. John Dilley's North American/Dilley #19 *Vendetta* was among the most eagerly anticipated contestants at Reno in 1988. Dilley, a fixed-based operator from Fort Wayne, Indiana, mated the wing (minus tiptanks) and horizontal stabilizer of a Learjet 23 bizjet to a Mustang fuselage and fin. [*Philip Wallick*]

LEFT Dubbed 'Learstang' by race aficionados, *Vendetta* is powered by a Jack Hovey-prepared Rolls-Royce Merlin 622. During tests prior to arrival at Reno Dilley reported a true airspeed of 475 mph at 80 inches of boost. 'It runs excellently, you can turn it on a dime. I did some "combat" with other Mustangs and I could turn right inside them every time. It rolls just like a Pitts Special. You just touch the stick and it starts rolling. Climbing out of Reno here at 5000 feet altitude I get a 4600 feet per minute rate of climb.' [*Philip Wallick*]

BELOW A backfire prior to qualifications runs kept *Vendetta* out of the running in 1988, but John Dilley is optimistic about its future. 'I feel the aircraft has definite potential. It's just at its starting point and its fast already. I feel it will easily go around the pylons at 470.' [*Philip Wallick*]

BELOW, RIGHT AND BELOW RIGHT Gary Levitz flew his stock P-51D Mustang # 38 *Miss Ashley* to first place in the Gold final at Reno 88, clocking 381.347 mph. Levitz, president of a retail furniture company, has been a regular Gold contender at Reno in a P-38 Lightning and Mustangs. He finds pylon racing relaxing. 'I'd rather fly all day around the pylons than I would fly through the Phoenix terminal control area once. I get more stressed out just going to work in the week than I do racing.'
[*Photographs by Philip Wallick*]

LEFT P-51 #86 *No Name Lady* was the mount of Delbert Williams in 1982. Having qualified eighth fastest, at 396.609 mph, Williams took the lead in the fifth lap of the first Silver heat and held it to the checkered flag. It was the first unlimited race he had ever flown. Williams's consistently strong performance in the heats put him in the Gold final, in which he again flew a fine race, placing third behind *Dago Red* and *Fat Cat*. [*Nigel Moll*]

BELOW Williams grew up and went to school with Joe Banducci, the owner of #86. Banducci took the airplane out of racing in 1980, but he and Williams got talking and decided to race. Bob Love, a veteran of the pylons, checked Williams out on the finer points of hurtling around at ground level with six other warbirds. [*Nigel Moll*]

BELOW Rookie Delbert Williams banks *No Name Lady* high around pylon 7 on his way to third place in the Gold final in 1982. [*Nigel Moll*]

PORTRAITS OF POWER

BELOW In 1988 the patriotic red, white and blue #11 *Miss America* was the mount of veteran Reno racer Chuck 'Always Second' Hall, whose duels in his P-51 #5 *Miss R J* with Darryl Greenamyer's Bearcat were a feature of Reno races in the 1960s. [*Philip Wallick*]

BELOW RIGHT Flown by ex-Royal Canadian Air Force pilot Bud Granley, a hard charger who left roostertails of desert dust with *Miss America*'s clipped wingtips, the Mustang reached the 1988 Gold final after a 420.287 mph win in Heat 2B, but was forced to retire after five laps of the Championship. [*Philip Wallick*]

BELOW Fly the flag. The former Howie Keef P-51D *Miss America* is now owned by Washington businessman Ron Smyth – who is blind, and has never seen his beautiful 'flying Old Glory'. [*Mike Jerram*]

PORTRAITS OF POWER

BELOW AND RIGHT No newcomer to Reno, *Georgia Mae* was formerly the late Jack Sliker's *Escape I*. The polished aluminum finish almost hurt your eyes in the clear Nevada air, and if it looks familiar, it should: owner Wiley Sanders, who runs a trucking company in Troy, Alabama, also owned the look alike *Jeannie*. In 1985 John Putman flew *Georgia Mae*, qualifying at 418 mph and recording 387 mph in Thursday and Friday's heats, but on Saturday, after leading throughout Heat 3B, he pulled off the power to save

Georgia's engine and let Lefty Gardner's P-51D *Thunderbird* slide through to win. In the landing *Georgia Mae* groundlooped in a gusting crosswind and was greviously damaged. [*Mike Jerram*]

BELOW RIGHT *Georgia Mae*, seen here being buffed up for the Gold final as owner Sanders (right) looks on, was *Jeannie*'s replacement in the Wiley Sanders Racing Team stable in 1988. Pilot John Putman placed fourth at 408.287. [*Philip Wallick*]

LEFT AND RIGHT Jim Orton, flying John Sandberg's #28 *Tipsy Too*, passed Bob Love in the Hovey Mustang just short of the home pylon and went onto win the Saturday Silver heat at 362.903 mph in 1982. Love finished fourth, just a shade slower at 360.098. [*Nigel Moll*]

BELOW George Roberts taxies out for a late-evening ride in Wiley Sanders' #96, *Jeannie*'s stablemate. #96 was the first Mustang built in Australia—hence the art on the left main gear door. Roberts won the Bronze final in 1982 and, at the subsequent awards banquet, he put his trophy to fine use by filling it with champagne. He brought some glory to the ill-fated *Jeannie* team. [*Nigel Moll*]

BELOW RIGHT Sanders' *Jeannie Too* was flown by Ron Hevle at Reno in 1988. [*Philip Wallick*]

PORTRAITS OF POWER

Skip Holm, Bob Love and Jim Orton jockey for the advantage between pylons six and seven in Friday's Silver heat at Reno 82. The three pilots finished in that order, each separated by half a second at the flag. [*Nigel Moll*]

ABOVE Jim Maloney flew the Bud Light Mustang #0, stablemate of the Bud Light Corsair, at Reno 82. He qualified at 362.446 mph and placed seventh at 334.834 in the Silver final. [*Nigel Moll*]

ABOVE RIGHT Despite *Jeannie*'s untimely departure from the field, Skip Holm got to race in 1982 by flying #68 *Shangri-La*, the only airworthy P-51B. Bob Love, rather than compete in his own Mustang, *Illegitimatus Non Carborundum*, flew #2, a P-51D owned by engine man Jack Hovey. The engine in #2 is a Merlin 622 out of a Canadair North Star and Hovey, by limiting race boost to stock power (1720 hp), hoped to see a TBO (time between overhaul) of 1400 hours. He likes to race his airplane not to win, but just for the fun of it. [*Nigel Moll*]

RIGHT P-51B #68 *Shangri-La* sips on a volatile cocktail: avgas 115–145, a brew that's now as rare as the antiques that consume it. A suitable quantity is shipped into Reno each year to quench the thirst of the Unlimiteds and any other visiting relics. [*Nigel Moll*]

ABOVE *The Healer*, one of the numerous P-51s at Reno, awaits the call for an Unlimited heat in 1987. The aircraft appears in more competition on pages 76–77. [*Philip Handleman*]

LEFT *The Healer* edging out *Ciao Bella*, the Fiat G.59-B of Australian Guido Zuccoli, in one of the Unlimited heats at Reno 87. [*Philip Handleman*]

BELOW #69 *Georgia Mae*, a P-51 Mustang flown by John Putman, was placed fourth in the 1988 Gold final. Wiley Sanders's aircraft is featured on pages 126–127. [*Philip Wallick*]

BOTTOM Bill Rheinschild's eye-hurting polished metal P-51D #45 *Risky Business* was the 1988 Silver winner at 414.495 mph – faster than the back markers in the Gold final. [*Philip Wallick*]

LEFT Overpowered by the heavier iron, the dainty P-40 Warhawk contributes a touch of charm and nostalgia to the Reno races. [*Philip Handleman*]

BELOW LEFT Clay Klabo in #85 *Fat Cat* streaks toward the checkered flag, second place and $16,374 in the Gold final at Reno 82. [*Nigel Moll*]

BELOW Tom Kelley's P-51D *Lou IV* suffered a pressure instrument failure during the Unlimited Heat 3B on 1985's Saturday, but was flying again on Sunday to take the Silver race at 374.418 mph. [*Mike Jerram*]

RIGHT His race number may be zilch, but John Maloney took fourth in the Unlimited Silver in P-51D *Spam Can* at Reno 85. [*Mike Jerram*]

'Numero Uno' – but a flatulent start for *Super Corsair* during its debut at the 1982 National Air Races, when it was sponsored by Budweiser beer and flown by Steve Hinton and the late Jim Maloney. For sheer brute force, the Maloney/Hinton Corsair was without equal at Reno 82: when those dormant pistons (28 of them) and spark plugs (56 of them) came alive and headed for the redline, they produced a staggering 3800 hp with water injection, but without the overboost that did wonders to a Merlin's power output. Although it looks like a Goodyear F2G, the Bud Light Corsair is actually an F4U-1 modified to be

similar to an F2G. The Pratt & Whitney R-4360 came out of a Douglas C-124 Globemaster, the 13-ft, 7-in diameter prop once pulled a Douglas Skyraider, and a pair of Grumman S-2 oil coolers with drag-reducing inlets took the heat off the lubricant. Pilot-owners Steve Hinton and Jim Maloney (Hinton of *Red Baron* fame, the P-51 that brushed 500 mph with the help of a Rolls-Royce Griffon and contra-rotating prop) severed 43 inches off each wing and faired off the outboard flaps in the quest for speed. [*Nigel Moll*]

PORTRAITS OF POWER

BELOW, BOTTOM AND RIGHT The Bud Light Corsair has a considerably hotter approach speed than a stock F2G – hotter by 5 kt – of 110 kt/130 mph. The cowling came off an A-26. The team, led by Maloney's father Ed, president of the Planes of Fame at Chino, California, built the Bud Corsair in four months using parts from various Corsair airframes. Before the races, Steve Hinton said that the airplane had been up to 450 mph in tests, using only 58 inches of the 70 inches of boost available. They were reluctant to boost the power over 58 because some aileron control problems had been encountered. With the original ailerons,

Hinton and Maloney were experiencing some snatch
at high speed, so they changed to new ailerons with a
larger Friese area for more bite. Hinton and Maloney
tossed a coin each day to decide who would fly the
Corsair or the Bud Light II P-51.
[*Photographs by Nigel Moll*]

LEFT AND BELOW Piston engines don't come any bigger than this Pratt & Whitney R-4360, the powerplant for the Hinton/Maloney Super Corsair. It has 28 cylinders, 28 pistons and 56 spark plugs in its four-row radial configuration. The 4360 stands for cubic inches' displacement: to put that figure in perspective, its cubic capacity is 71 litres or, put another way, 42 Volkswagen Rabbit/Golf engines. The 4360 in the Hinton and Maloney/Bud Light Corsair put out about 4000 hp, twice the power available to Corsairs of World War 2. According to pilot Jim Maloney, the airplane burns fuel at a rate of 400 gallons per hour at race speed and low altitude. The water-injection system runs at 100 gallons per hour. Just as the Bud Corsair is a highly modified F4U, so the original Vought-Goodyear F2G was a similar adaptation of the F4U, produced in response

to a US Navy requirement for a more powerful Corsair. Only ten F2Gs were built, however, because the cessation of World War 2 brought production to an end. Although Hinton and Maloney's Corsair is registered as a Vought-Goodyear F2G, it is considerably modified from wartime factory standard. At Reno 82, the airplane's first outing, it put on a fine performance: Steve Hinton qualified the airplane at 413.208 mph, and in the Unlimited Gold final he came in fourth at 362.496. [*Nigel Moll*]

RIGHT AND BELOW Few pilots nowadays get to sit behind a snout like the *Super Corsair*'s: Jim Maloney and Steve Hinton tossed a coin for the privilege each day in 1982. Despite the antiquity of the airframe and engine, the instrument panel was every inch up to date. [*Nigel Moll*]

PORTRAITS OF POWER

BELOW *Super Corsair*, now without beer backing, basks in late afternoon sunlight–and glory–in front of the Reno grandstands after taking the 1985 Unlimited championship. [*Mike Jerram*]

RIGHT Victorious Steve Hinton comes into land after securing his second Reno win. [*Mike Jerram*]

BELOW RIGHT Hinton speaks to the media. He still wasn't sure that he'd won as he taxied up to crowd center, but was soon in little doubt. 'It's always good to be the underdog,' he said. And even better to be the winner. [*Mike Jerram*]

RIGHT After several years as bridesmaid, the Planes of Fame Museum's Chino-based *Super Corsair* finally took first spot at Reno in 1985, albeit thanks to Neil Anderson's only slip in four days of racing. *Super Corsair* is powered by a 4360-cubic inch, 26-cylinder, four-row Pratt & Whitney R-4360 radial engine driving a Douglas Skyraider propeller. Power output is around 3800 hp. Fuel consumption? If you have to ask you can't afford it, but figure on 400 US gallons per hour at race speeds. Steve Hinton clocked 438.186 mph for the Gold final, setting a new Reno race record and giving the Corona, California-based pilot his first Reno victory since 1978, when he took the Unlimited Championship in the RB-51 *Red Baron*. He nearly died a year later in the desert crash which followed an engine seizure and totally demolished the much-modified, Griffon-engined Mustang. Hinton took the Championship after trailing Neil Anderson in the Sanders Super Sea Fury *Dreadnought* for the entire race. Anderson, distracted by a temperature gauge, cut the final pylon turn heading for the checkered flag and gave Hinton the sole Corsair victory in Reno's 25-year history. 'Winning in the Corsair was special because it's fun winning being the underdog . . . nobody expected us to do it and it was great, fantastic!' he recalls. [*Mike Jerram*]

BELOW Part of the Reno ritual is for each Unlimited racer's crew to tow their aircraft in front of the grandstands in a ceremony just prior to the last and most important heat – the Unlimited Gold. Here John Maloney gets the royal treatment in 1987 as his crew tows his *Super Corsair*, a former champion. The name of brother Jim, who died in the crash of an antique Ryan trainer in which he was a passenger, is retained on #1 as a tribute. [*Philip Handleman*]

LEFT Steve Hinton turns towards Reno Gold in 1985. 'It's a real sense of satisfaction and gratification when you work on these airplanes and compete, to get the maximum performance you can . . . There are moments of apprehension and wondering if you should be doing it, but when it's all over it's worth doing it. Winning is great.' [*Mike Jerram*]

BELOW LEFT Ed Maloney's Chino-based Planes of Fame Museum took a stock F4U Corsair and grafted a 28-cylinder four-row Pratt & Whitney R-4360 onto it, recreating the shape and sound of the monster F2G-1s in which Cook Cleland and Ben McKillen dominated the postwar Thompson Trophy races at Cleveland. However, the fatal crash in 1949 of Bill Odom's heavily modified P-51C Mustang *Beguine* put an end to Unlimited air racing in the United States for 15 years – until the revival at Reno under Bill Stead in 1964. [*Philip Wallick*]

BELOW # 1's 13 ft 7 in ex-Douglas Skyraider prop disappears in a shimmering arc as its crew chief runs up the R-4360 prior to a heat race at Reno 88. John Maloney was in the hot seat. John qualified *Super Corsair* at 447.319 mph, but had finished only seven laps when Sunday's final ended. What was it like the first time he flew the 3800 hp charger? 'I don't know. I was too busy hanging on!' [*Philip Wallick*]

F4U-4 #101, owned and flown by Bob Yancey, has a
DC-7 spinner around the hub of its big four-blade
propeller for a whisker more speed and better cooling.
[*Nigel Moll*]

ABOVE LEFT Santa Monica attorney Bob Guildford is a veteran campaigner in his stock F4U-7 Corsair #93 *Blue Max*, seen here taxiing in after finishing ninth (and last) in the 1985 Unlimited Bronze event. Speed: 282.904 mph. [*Nigel Moll*]

LEFT Bob Yancey's F4U-4 Corsair #101 *Old Blue* prepares for Unlimited heat 1B, which turned into a six-lap duel between Yancey and Dennis Sanders in Sea Fury #924 and provided some of the most exciting racing of the '85 event. [*Mike Jerram*]

ABOVE Yancey's Thursday battle with Dennis Sanders during Unlimited heat 1B was a high spot of the 1985 Reno races. Yancey took his F4U-4 Corsair *Old Blue* from last place to beat Sanders' Sea Fury #924 by just .22 of a second. 'It was kinda exciting,' he allowed modestly. *Old Blue* took second place in Sunday's Silver final, clocking 374.392 mph. [*Mike Jerram*]

ABOVE 'We came here to beat a Bearcat,' said Yancey, and ate up the entire field in Heat 1B. His pit crew quickly applied Sea Fury and Bearcat Kill markings to *Old Blue*'s flanks. [*Mike Jerram*]

ABOVE The Corsairs made for good variety around the pylons at Reno in 1982. This one, #82 *Wart Hog*, was flown by Mike Wright, of the Casper, Wyoming, Tired Iron Racing team. It qualified at 304.038 mph, compared with 333.433 mph and 346.861 mph by the two other F4Us flown, respectively, by Bob Guilford and Bob Yancey. [*Mike Jerram*]

ABOVE RIGHT Although an old Corsair is hardly suited to instrument flying, there's no harm in having a full complement of new instruments and avionics to keep track of Old Hose Nose's progress, pulse and position, as here on *Wart Hog*. [*Mike Jerram*]

RIGHT Completely restored by the Tired Iron team, *Wart Hog* is flown as both a warbird and as an unlimited air racer, though participating in a leisurely manner. This fighter is also equipped with gas-operated 'machine-gun'–units that give off a noise convincingly like .50 caliber Brownings and, needless to say, extremely popular with airshow crowds. [*Mike Jerram*]

BELOW AND INSET Dallas real estate developer Alan Preston brought his 1984 championship winning Mustang *Stiletto*, a Harvard trainer and his F4U-5NL Corsair #12 *Old Deadeye* to the Reno races in 1985. [*Mike Jerram*]

BELOW Going into the chute for the start of the first Unlimited heat of the 1985 National Championship Air Races, *Old Deadeye*'s canopy suddenly exploded. 'It sounded like a quarter stick of dynamite going off. I don't know if I hit a bird or what,' declared a supercool Bruce Lockwood after a hurried landing. A substitute canopy and some patching of the fin and stabilizer got *Old Deadeye* into racing trim again by Sunday, when it placed sixth in the Bronze division. [*Mike Jerram*]

ABOVE The Corsair, a former night-fighter variant racing minus the starboard wing radar pod which it wore in US Navy service, was flown in 1985 by its former owner Bruce Lockwood. Here the distinctive aircraft poses in profile against the Nevada skyline. [*Mike Jerram*]

One of the more precious pieces of metal at Reno in 1982 was Lloyd Hamilton's immaculate Hawker Sea Fury #16 *Baby Gorilla*, here glowing in the desert dusk in its Australian colors. [*Nigel Moll*]

Above *Baby Gorilla* was raced at Reno in 1988 by corporate pilot C. J. Stephens of Santa Rosa, California. He placed third in the Bronze event at 386.869 mph. [*Philip Wallick*]

LEFT The authentic colors of the Royal Australian Navy had a modification to the fuselage roundel for 1988—the addition of race sponsors Camel cigarettes' logo. [*Philip Wallick*]

RIGHT Lloyd Hamilton rounding a pylon on the Reno course. Like most Gold racers Hamilton is happiest in the close company of his peers, and enjoys the great camaraderie of Unlimited racing, but 'There's no such thing as camaraderie once the pace plane pulls up. If you're not aggressive, you're not out there to win.' [*Philip Wallick*]

BELOW LEFT Lloyd Hamilton's *Baby Gorilla* qualified at 381.467 mph in 1982 by making its solo run around the course in 1:26.7. The Sea Fury is as different from a P-51 in sound as in looks: while the P-51s run tortured from gross overboost and overspeed, the Fury and its Bristol Centaurus two-row radial sigh around the pylons with a deep, rumbling whoosh. The aircraft seemed most relaxed about the whole wild business of racing. [*Nigel Moll*]

BELOW The Sea Fury represented the end of an era for the Royal Navy. It was the last (and to many the most beautiful) piston-engined fighter to serve with the Fleet Air Arm. The airplane packs a 2480-hp Bristol Centaurus with 18 cylinders. With a wing area of just 280 square feet and a gross weight of 12,500 lb, the Sea Fury has a top speed of 460 mph at 18,000 feet. [*Nigel Moll*]

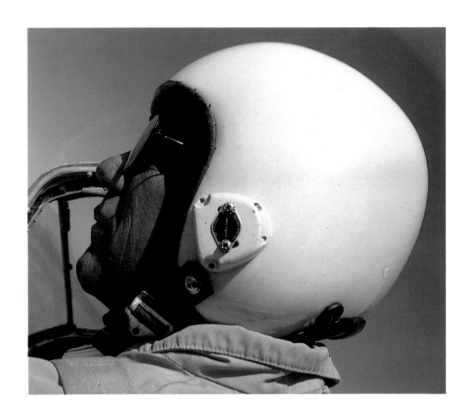

BELOW *Baby Gorilla* and Skip Holm in *Blind Man's Bluff* at Reno 87. [*Philip Handleman*]

RIGHT Flying Tiger Line captain Richard Drury made his Reno debut in Sea Fury #43 at Reno 85 and took second in the Bronze division at 345.903 mph. [*Mike Jerram*]

RIGHT There's no restriction on parking space on the Reno ramp, but Flying Tigers captain Richard Drury still chooses to fold away the wings of his #43 Sea Fury, which wears authentic early postwar Fleet Air Arm colors. Clark gained sixth spot in the Silver division at 356.736 mph. [*Mike Jerram*]

LEFT The late Frank Sanders, long-time exponent of the British Hawker Sea Fury, hit on the idea of re-engining the 2480 hp Bristol Centaurus-powered fighter with a 3800 hp Pratt & Whitney R-4360-63A 'corncob' and first brought the meticulously prepared *Dreadnought* to Reno in 1983. Flown by General Dynamics famed F-16 test pilot Neil Anderson in his rookie racing year, #8 *Dreadnought* almost loafed through qualification at 446.39 mph and took Gold at 425.24 mph after a ding-dong battle with Rick Brickert in P-51 *Dago Red*, who had to call a 'Mayday' on lap 6. [*Philip Wallick*]

BELOW AND BOTTOM *Dreadnought* was originally a Sea Fury T.20 two-seat fighter-trainer delivered to Burma, from where it was recovered in 1979. Apart from the corncob R-4360-63A engine grafted onto its nose and 13 ft 6 in Aeroproducts four-blade propeller, *Dreadnought* has an extended vertical fin and rudder for increased directional stability and a meticulously cleaned up airframe; 115/145 octane racing brew goes into port wing and fuselage tanks. Frank's Air Racing Team (colloquially known by the unflattering acronym FART) claim a maximum level speed in excess of 490 mph. [*Mike Jerram*]

ABOVE LEFT Rick Brickert chases Bill Destefani's P-51 *Strega* in vain during 1987's Gold final. [*Philip Wallick*]

LEFT Airline pilot Rick Brickert took over from Neil Anderson as *Dreadnought*'s pilot in 1986 and took Gold that year at 434.488 mph. In 1988 he qualified third fastest at 458.920 mph and chased Gold winner Lyle Shelton all the way to the line, with a race speed of 451.202 mph. Brickert, who dreamed of flying at Reno ever since his sister brought him to the races at the age of 13, is impressed by the reliability of the corncob Sea Fury and its lack of 'cockpit complexity'. 'Coming down the chute I close the doors up, at 40 inches of boost I turn on the ADI, turn on the cylinder head spray system and go all the way up. After that it's just a question of monitoring it while concentrate on racing.' [*Philip Wallick*]

ABOVE Streaming vapor from underwing radiator spraybars, the Sanders Super Sea Fury *Dreadnought* lived up to its name in 1985, consistently leading the Unlimited field throughout the heat races, with a fastest speed of 436.947 mph on Saturday. Next day pilot Neil Anderson again led the pack from the outset, harried but never quite caught by Steve Hinton in *Super Corsair*. Then, rounding the final pylon on the last lap of the Gold final, Anderson cut inside the turn. Though he took the checkered flag, race officials penalized him 16 seconds for the cut giving the Championship to Hinton, who was just four seconds behind. 'I was watching a temperature gauge and suddenly the pylon wasn't there,' admitted F-16 test pilot Anderson. 'You just get too busy.' The marvelous aircraft is also featured, in its display role, on pages 26–27. [*Mike Jerram*]

LEFT, RIGHT AND BELOW In addition to *Baby Gorilla* Lloyd Hamilton's Santa Rosa, California-based racing team fielded another Sea Fury, *Furias*, in 1985, which made its Reno debut as *Head Gorilla* in 1983, then failed to reach the finals in 1984 after losing most of its cowling during a heat race. The 28-cylinder, four-row R-4360 engine, popularly known as the 'corncob', put out some 3800 hp against the Bristol Centaurus' 2480 hp; and, unlike the $50,000 race-prepared Rolls-Royce Merlins demanded by the P-51 racers, the old corncobs could be had for $4000 or so. [*Photographs by Mike Jerram*]

LEFT *Furias'* big banger, turning a Skyraider propeller, took Lloyd Hamilton to 411.952 mph and fourth place in the Unlimited Gold race at Reno 85. [*Mike Jerram*]

BOTTOM Color me quick. Hamilton's team could wear anything they liked so long as it was red, to match the sanguine shade of *Furias'* flanks. [*Mike Jerram*]

RIGHT *Furias* qualified at 424.081 mph in 1988 and placed fifth in the Gold final after overtaking John Maloney in *Super Corsair*. [*Philip Wallick*]

BELOW LEFT AND BELOW The sleek 'corncob' Sea Fury #15 *Furias* has undergone continual refinement since its debut as *Head Gorilla* in 1983 – including addition of sponsor's logo – but has so far been denied Gold. [*Photographs by Philip Wallick*]

PORTRAITS OF POWER

Boat manufacturer Dale Clark from Covina, California, went down among the sagebrush in 1985 in his two-seat Sea Fury #40 *Nuthin Special*, battling hard with Howard Pardue's F8F-1 Bearcat in Unlimited Heat 3C. The Bearcat finally got the better of him, taking first at 356.087 mph. The close companionship continued in the Silver fly-off, with Clark finishing just three miles per hour behind fifth-placed Pardue. [*Mike Jerram*]

LEFT Clean bear: Howard Pardue's rare short fin F8F-1 Bearcat #14 waxed its way into fifth place in the Unlimited Silver division at Reno 85 with a race speed of 359.415 mph. [*Mike Jerram*]

LEFT AND RIGHT Lyle Shelton's modified F8F-2 Bearcat #77 *Rare Bear* won at Reno in 1973 as the *7¼% Special*, and again in 1975 as the *Aircraft Cylinder Special*. The huge ex-Skyraider propeller demands near three-point take-offs and landings. At the 1985 races *Rare Bear* was flown by local Sparks, Nevada, man and former Lear Fan test pilot John Penney, making his debut in the event. Penney's race speed in Thursday's Heat 1A was 407.502 mph, putting the Bearcat among the fancied contenders for Gold. Alas . . . [*Mike Jerram*]

LEFT Dirty bear: during the Friday Gold division heat Penney called a 'Mayday' and pulled up, streaming white vapor. A missing safety wire on an oil plug had allowed the *Rare Bear*'s lifeblood to be pumped overboard. After pulling off an exceptionally skilful deadstick landing in an aeroplane with the gliding characteristics of a concrete slab, Penney slithered off *Rare Bear*'s oil-washed wing roots to discover the engine totally seized. [*Mike Jerram*]

RIGHT Bear pit: #77's cockpit is workmanlike spartan. The purple control column is a legacy from *Rare Bear*'s previous paint scheme. What's it like in there during a race? Shelton explains: 'When you get up above 440 mph it's a real hostile environment. It's hot – before we did a cooling job it used to get so hot that I could hardly keep my feet on the rudder pedals – and the noise and vibration and the clamor is just mind-boggling. The stick forces are high, you need about all of your strength, two hands, to make turns, and you're just as busy as you can be and the adrenalin is high because you're just on the hairline edge of destruction of these engines. I used to be an amateur boxer, which is a pretty physical sport, but after a race I come back feeling like I've been in a five-round fight.' [*Philip Wallick*]

LEFT Here's a man just minutes away from becoming National Air Race Champion. Dallas-based Lyle Shelton, a former US Navy pilot and old campaigner at Reno, twice winner of the Unlimited Class Championship in 1973 and 1975, saddles up for the start of the 1988 Gold final. His victory brought him a bonus cheque of $10,000 from new Unlimited race sponsors RJ Reynolds Tobacco Co., and Shelton came away $40,437 richer after his win – no fortune when set against the immense cost of maintaining a competitive Unlimited air racer. Shelton and *Rare Bear* were back again for Reno 89 to record a sensational fourth Gold victory. [*Philip Wallick*]

LEFT AND BELOW After qualifying at a blistering new closed course record speed of 474.622 mph in 1988, Shelton and *Rare Bear* quickly took the lead of the Gold final pack, completing the eight-lap course in 9:38.18 for a race average of 456.821 mph. 'I looked back at the Bearcat and he was about six feet behind me and then he just accelerated by me like a shot,' said second place man Rick Brickert, whose Super Sea Fury *Dreadnought* finished seven seconds behind. [*Philip Wallick*]

BOTTOM *Rare Bear* heads for the start, trailed by John Maloney in the 1985 winner *Super Corsair*. Lyle Shelton bought the Bearcat as a derelict wreck for $2500 in the spring of 1968, restored it, installed a 3800 hp Wright R-3350 that 'spat out sand, leaves, trash, mice and bugs' the first time he ran it, and was placed fifth in the Championship final in 1969. Shelton and the 'Cat have been regular competitors at Reno ever since – four-time winners of Unlimited gold. [*Philip Wallick*]

PORTRAITS OF POWER

Minneapolis industrialist John Sandberg's *Tsunami*, seen here in 1986, is the only wholly original design Unlimited racer to have appeared at Reno in its 27-year history. Sandberg, who has been involved with the preparation of racers for a quarter of a century, set out to build the world's fastest piston-engined airplane. He enlisted the help of designer Bruce Boland, a Lockheed aerodynamicist whose influence can be seen in many Unlimited racers, along with Pete Law, Ray Poe and Tom Emery, and work began in 1979. [*Philip Wallick*]

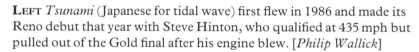

LEFT *Tsunami* (Japanese for tidal wave) first flew in 1986 and made its Reno debut that year with Steve Hinton, who qualified at 435 mph but pulled out of the Gold final after his engine blew. [*Philip Wallick*]

ABOVE AND ABOVE LEFT *Tsunami* came to Reno 88 much modified from previous years. The JRS team rebuilt the airframe, replacing the entire back end with a magnesium structure, resulting in a weight reduction of some 700 lb. New water and oil cooling systems, new inlet scoop and outlet door, more downthrust for the engine, increased fin and rudder area, new ten-foot diameter propeller, trimmable stabilizer and revised aileron controls were just some of the modifications. Pilot Steve Hinton expressed himself well pleased with #18's handling. He qualified second fastest in the Unlimited field at 470.899 mph, pipped *Dreadnought* to the line in Saturday's Heat 3A with a course record 462.218 mph, but suffered a coolant valve failure in the Gold final and was forced to throttle back, placing third at a race speed of 429.947 mph. [*Philip Wallick*]

BELOW Wide-eyed with wonder: *Tsunami* fabrication man Don Pennington. Designer Bruce Boland's brief was to create the smallest possible airframe to fit behind the engine, which is built up from a Rolls-Royce/Packard V-1650-7 crankcase and two-stage blower with heavy duty crankshaft and cylinder head and bank assemblies from the Merlin 624 and 724 series used on postwar transport aircraft. Maximum racing output is around 3600 hp at 105 inches of boost. Boland certainly succeeded in his task: *Tsunami* has a frontal area 77% of that of stock P-51, and at 146 square its wing area is only 60% of the Mustang's. [*Philip Wallick*]

LEFT AND BELOW Apart from the wing shape you would never guess that Joe Betty Kasperoff's #97 *Mr Awesome* started life as timeworn Soviet-designed Yakolev Yak-11 two-seat trainer (NATO codename *Moose*). Some 4566 Yak-11s were built in the Soviet Union and Czechoslovakia between 1946 and 1956. Kasperoff had his ex-Egyptian Air Force Yak totally reconfigured in great secrecy at Van Nuys Airport, California, its 680 hp Shvetsov Ash-21 radial engine replaced by a monstrous Wright R-3350 with three turbochargers and a blower driving a ten-foot four-blade propeller. On the test stand the R-3350 put out 3750 hp, and was believed to be producing 3500 hp at

Reno 88. Two-times Reno Gold Champion and Lockheed test pilot Skip Holm was flying the beast, and commented prior to racing: 'The Yak is back to bare bones 1930s airframe. You could send it back in time 40 years to the Jimmy Doolittle days and that airplane would look at home.' And like the Gee Bees of the Golden Age *Mr Awesome* proved to be quite a handful. 'The Yak is the closest I've ever come to not feeling a part of the machine,' observed Holm. 'I guess the first time I thought an airplane was going to hurt me I wouldn't fly it.' [*Philip Wallick*]

PORTRAITS OF POWER

BOTTOM Oregon-based cropduster and veteran Reno campaigner Bob Yancey, best known for his F4U-4 Corsair *Old Blue*, has also caught Yak fever, but his #101 is less drastically modified than *Mr Awesome*. Re-engined with a Pratt & Whitney R-2800 driving a four-blade propeller made up of blades from a North American T-28 trainer set in a Bearcat hub assembly, the craft was one of two 'basket case' Yak-11s which Yancey acquired from a batch of former Egyptian Air Force aircraft in late 1986. After making his debut with the Yak in 1987, Yancey came back to Reno in 1988 'to give someone a run for the money,' qualified at 373.766 mph and placed fourth in the Silver final at 386.515 mph. [*Philip Wallick*]

RIGHT 'You do not have a Yak,' Soviet officials told British aircraft restorer Doug Bianchi when he asked them for help in rebuilding this Russian Yak-11 trainer rescued from a dump after a forced landing on Cyprus. Oh yes he did, and what's more he completed the rebuild without their help. The Yak later caused a stir at a USAF base in Britain, when Neil Williams landed unannounced with an engine problem, and it's now resident in the US. [*Mike Jerram*]

BELOW Skip Holm qualified *Mr Awesome* at 417.272 mph – but declined to race again after a violent pitch-up in Heat 2B. [*Philip Wallick*]

BELOW A newcomer to Reno in 1987 was *Maniyak*, a newly rebuilt Soviet Yak-11 from the Egyptian Air Force. Not considered a serious contender in the Unlimited class's Gold heat, this Yak experienced mechanical difficulties that grounded it during the races. Nevertheless, its sleek lines and bright red paint job added a lot of color and beauty to Reno's flight line. [*Philip Handleman*]

BOTTOM Ready to race! This silver Yak-11 also belongs to Unlimited racer Bob Yancey and sports a very powerful 'Pratt'. [*Philip Handleman*]

LEFT Reno is about more than just the brute power or the Unlimiteds: AT-6s/SNJs (Harvards) have a class of their own. Although slower than the P-51s, the AT-6s make a fine spectacle as they battle around the pylons to the rasp of transonic prop tips. Ralph Twombly cleaned up in the class at Reno in 1982. He qualified fastest, at 219.245 mph, and went on to win the Gold final at 214.9 mph. The Gold final carried a $20,000 purse, $4500 of which went to Twombly when he took the checkered flag. His steed was #44 *Miss Behavin'*, which has a long history. [*Nigel Moll*]

BELOW LEFT Jerry McDonald was the fourth fastest qualifier in #5 *Big Red* at Reno 82. He took seventh and last position in the Gold final, at 204.983 mph. [*Nigel Moll*]

BOTTOM LEFT San Joaquin, California ag pilot Jerry McDonald bought his SNJ-4 *Big Red* 'on a whim' in 1978. He took the AT-6 class Silver race at Reno 85, narrowly beating Alan Preston in old campaigner #44, *Miss Behavin'*, with a race speed of 216.236 mph. [*Mike Jerram*]

BELOW Jimmy Gist's signwriter had another line to add to *Texas Red*'s tally shortly after this picture was taken: '1985 4th Gold Div. 209.071 mph'. [*Mike Jerram*]

BOTTOM *Texas Red* is one of the more colorful AT-6s racing today. After a two-year hiatus, the AT-6s/SNJs returned to Reno in 1981 with their own special course. It was in 1978 that two airplanes collided while racing on the small Formula One circuit, with the loss of two pilots' lives. From 1981, the old trainers had their own five-mile circuit; in 1978 they had used the Formulas' 3.108-mile course. The larger course, while still making for an exciting race, gave the airplanes plenty of space. [*Nigel Moll*]

LEFT AND BELOW Bill and Bud Arnot had a matched pair of racers at Reno for 1985: T-6 *Silver Baby* took sixth place in the Silver division, flown by Charles Hutchins of Texas City, and their B-25J Mitchell *Silver Lady* cruised around the course but failed to qualify. [*Mike Jerram*]

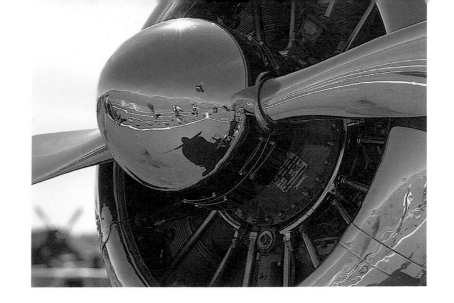

RIGHT AND BELOW No engine or airframe modifications are permitted in the AT-6/SNJ class at Reno, but always among the best prepared and glossiest contenders is Al Goss' SNJ-6 *Warlock*, 'Quick Son of a Witch', which was runner-up in the 1985 Gold final at 213.682 mph. [*Mike Jerram*]

LEFT Charlie Beck's SNJ-4 *Honest Entry* acquired a prop tip and cowling 'kill' marking in addition to its pylon-hugging logo after it nosed over. [*Mike Jerram*]

BELOW During a challenging at Reno in 1987 contest Beck, in the striped tail SNJ-4, and Bruce Redding, in his red AT-6, appear to be flying formation. [*Philip Handleman*]

BOTTOM Bruce Redding's Texan and Nick Macy's *Six Cat* battle for position in 1987. Racing in the AT-6 class is often Reno's most exciting category because the airplanes are so evenly matched. [*Philip Handleman*]

LEFT AND BELOW Charlie Beck, a building contractor from Olivenhain, California, really had his nose rubbed in it in 1985. The 62-year-old veteran combat pilot, who flew 68 World War 2 missions in P-47s and P-51s, pulled out of Heat 1C on Thursday with a suspected loose propeller blade. Proving the old adage that a T-6 is never safely landed until it is tied down, he put *Honest Entry* onto its nose while attempting to correct an incipient groundloop. Beck was unhurt and with new propeller, cowl and help from fellow T-6 racers, *Honest Entry* was back in the air two days later. [*Mike Jerram*]

PORTRAITS OF POWER

BELOW With their own special class, the Racing Biplanes were set apart from the stock Sport Biplanes at Reno 82, making for fairer racing and some close battles at the pylons. *Sundancer*'s Midget Mustang heritage can be seen as the airplane hitches a tail-first ride across the ramp in preparation for a racehose start onto the course. [*Nigel Moll*]

BOTTOM If it hadn't been for Don Beck's *Sorceress*, there probably would be no racing Biplane class. When *Sorceress* appeared in 1968, she met all the formula criteria for the Sport Biplane class but was 50 mph faster than the other contenders – aircraft such as the Pitts Special, Mong Sport and Starduster. For five years, the Sport Biplane pilots had to be content

with second place to *Sorceress* and Don Beck, but in 1973 *Sundancer* (left), developed by Sid White from the homebuilt Midget Mustang, appeared and toppled Beck. These two 'super biplanes' dominated the field, and the other pilots cried 'foul'. In 1980 another challenger entered the fray, *Cobra*. All three were at Reno 82: Don Beck and *Sorceress*, Pat Hines with *Sundancer* and Al Kramer with *Cobra*, along with two others – Dan Mortensen in the Amsoil/Rutan tandem-wing special and Tom Aberle in #25 *Two Bits*. All five raced in their own Racing Division of the Biplane class, and their speeds ranged from 202 to 223 mph in qualifying, with Pat Hines in *Sundancer* fastest. Hines also took the Gold, at 209.401 mph, closely followed by Mortensen at 209.206 and Beck at 206.289. Kramer pulled *Cobra* out of the race in the final lap after being lapped. [*Nigel Moll*]

RIGHT Dennis Brown hitched a video camera onto the fin of Pitts Special #29 *Scarlet*, which he qualified at 147.958 mph and flew into sixth place in the Gold final at 143.171 mph. The Gold final was flown in some of the worst conditions thrown at Reno 82, with rain and dim visibility. [*Nigel Moll*]

BELOW Firmly in the Rutan mould, the Amsoil/Rutan Special qualified second fastest in 1982 at 212.327 mph, flown by Dan Mortensen of Superior, Wisconsin. Mortensen finished second in the Gold final, just 0.2 mph and 0.3 seconds behind winner Pat Hines in *Sundancer*. [*Nigel Moll*]

ABOVE LEFT Construction engineer Dennis Brown had a video camera mounted on the centre section handgrip of Pitts #29 *Scarlet*, and filmed himself en route to third place in the Biplane Silver event in 1985. [*Mike Jerram*]

LEFT AND BELOW The two Dons, Fairbanks and Beck, are old campaigners in the Biplane class with Knight Twister Imperial #5 *White Knight* and the much modified Smith Miniplane #00 *Miss Lake Tahoe* respectively. In 1985, 61-year-old Fairbanks, who set a Sport Biplane class qualifying record at Reno a year earlier, was just 0.9 mph behind 63-year-old Beck in Heat 1A, but in Sunday's Gold final *Miss Lake Tahoe* won at 195.623 mph, with *White Knight* second at 177.665 mph. 'Dedication and concentration are the keys to winning,' said five times Biplane champ Beck. [*Mike Jerram*]

ABOVE Very punny: Earl Allen's *Pitts-n-Pieces* was the fastest of the Pitts Specials in the Biplane Class in 1985. Pilot Del Schulte took it to 144.703 mph and fifth place in the Gold division. While it is inevitable that the Unlimiteds draw the most attention and crowds at Reno, the IFM/Formula Ones and Racing Biplanes are actually purer racers, designed solely for the purpose of being first over the finishing line. In contrast to the heavyweights, they buzz around their own, tighter course like garish insects – yet still pursued by the same desire to be first that drives the heavy metal. [*Mike Jerram*]

GOOD GUYS

LEFT AND BELOW The Fairey Swordfish torpedo bomber was an anachronism when World War 2 broke out, yet served courageously throughout the conflict and outlasted its intended successor. Popularly known as the Stringbag – not for its bestrutted, wire-braced airframe, but because it could carry 'more stores than a lady could fit into her stringbag on a shopping trip' – the unlikely looking biplane was responsible for sinking a greater tonnage of enemy shipping than any other Allied aircraft. This example is the only airworthy Swordfish, flown regularly by the Fleet Air Arm Historic Flight. [*Mike Jerram*]

GOOD GUYS

RIGHT AND BELOW RIGHT The Fleet Air Arm Historic Flight's Sea Fury FB.11 served in the Korean War with No 807 Squadron aboard the aircraft-carrier HMS *Theseus*, flying 200 operational sorties before retirement in 1954. Manufacturers Hawker returned the aircraft to the Royal Navy in 1971 for complete restoration to airworthiness, and it carries authentic markings worn during the Korean campaign. The Sea Fury was the last of the Fleet Air Arm's propeller-driven fighters and with a maximum speed in full military trim of 460 mph lays claim to being the fastest production single-engined piston fighter; stripped Sea Furies in racing trim have exceeded 520 mph in the US. The complexities of the sleeve-valve Centaurus engine have inspired several conversions to Pratt & Whitney radials. [*Mike Jerram*]

FAR RIGHT Conceived as a lightweight redesign of the Tempest, the Hawker Fury was rejected by the RAF and adapted for shipboard service with the Fleet Air Arm as the Sea Fury, powered by a 2550-hp Bristol Centaurus 18-cylinder sleeve-valve engine driving a five-bladed propeller. Roughly equivalent to the US Navy's Bearcat, though rather more stable as a gun platform, the Sea Fury saw action during the Korean War and is credited with the destruction of a MiG-15 when a Communist pilot strayed within range of No 802 Squadron Fleet Air Arm pilot Lt Peter Carmichael's four 20 mm cannon. The two-seat Sea Fury T.20 pictured here was a trainer version. [*Mike Jerram*]

ABOVE The 'torpedo' on the Fairey Swordfish is a dummy, doubling as a handy baggage container for airshow trips away from its base at the Royal Naval Air Station, Yeovilton, Somerset, England. For the benefit of those who might wonder, this photographer can confirm that the Stringbag's open cockpit is *c-o-l-d*, even on a balmy spring day. Imagine what it must have been like operating off a carrier in winter up near the Arctic Circle – or perhaps you would rather not. [*Mike Jerram*]

The De Havilland Tiger Moth, cobbled together from parts of other Moths to meet a British Air Ministry specification in 1931, developed into one of the world's best-known training biplanes.

Remarkably young RAF pilots often found themselves in the cockpit of a Spitfire after too few hours in the less sophisticated trainer. Both aircraft are classics of their kind, the Tiger Moth gentle and

forgiving but with a knack of emphasizing every sloppy piloting habit, the Spitfire (see overleaf) slippery and knife-sharp with handling rarely matched and joyously rewarding to the skilled touch.

Surplus Tigers sold post-war for £50 apiece; restored examples such as this one, bearing wartime training camouflage, now carry price tags of £20,000 or more. [*Mike Jerram*]

ABOVE AND ABOVE RIGHT The instantly recognizable elliptical wing planform of the Spitfire is a visual delight – and a manufacturing headache. Unlike its simple 1920s-technology contemporary the Hawker Hurricane, the Spitfire, with its stressed skin monocoque fuselage, complex curvatures and subtlety of line, was ill-suited to the kind of mass production which was necessary in wartime. It has been estimated that each Spitfire took about 330,000 man-hours to manufacture – about three average working lifetimes. Total production ran to more than 20,000 in two dozen major marks. This aircraft is the RAF Battle of Britain Memorial Flight's Mark Vb. [*Mike Jerram*]

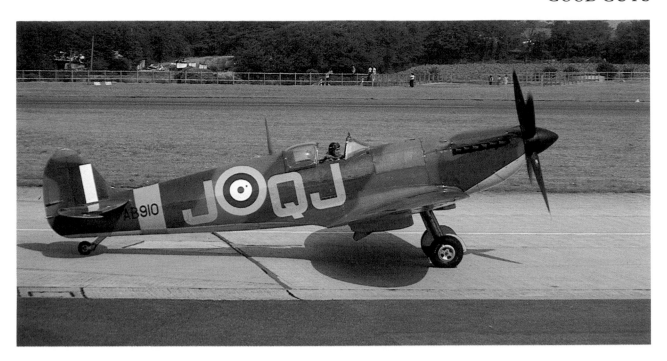

ABOVE 'Just the sort of bloody silly name they would choose,' sniffed Reginald Mitchell when told of the British Air Ministry's choice of Spitfire for his new fighter. Mitchell died before the aircraft entered RAF service and could scarcely have guessed the impact which his aeroplane was to have on world history, or the affection with which it's remembered. The Mark IX is arguably the best-handling of all marks of Spitfire; this one, owned by a consortium led by former Red Arrows team leader Ray Hanna, fetched £260,000 at an auction in 1983 and is preserved in full aerobatic condition. It was naturally in demand during 1990 as the RAF celebrated the golden anniversary of aerial victory over Germany in the Battle of Britain. [*Mike Jerram*]

ABOVE More than half a century after its first flight the perennial Douglas DC-3 Dakota soldiers on with cargo haulers and air forces the world over. Few are as lovingly cared for as Tom Thomas Jr's C-47 Skytrain transport in US Army Air Corps colors, operated by the Confederate Air Force. [*Mike Jerram*]

ABOVE LEFT An invasion-striped C-47 departs on a pleasure flying detail from Harlingen. [*Norman Pealing*]

LEFT Many aircraft manufacturers have tried to design a 'DC-3 replacement': the Vickers Viking, Saab Scandia, Handley Page Herald, Fokker Friendship and Avro 748 spring to mind. But nobody has ever really cracked the DC-3's secret. Today, even reworked turboprop versions—including one with three engines—are available and certificated. This is *Draggin' Lady*, resplendent in Army Air Corps uniform, waiting at Harlingen. [*Norman Pealing*]

RIGHT DC-3s by the yard at Abbotsford, British Columbia, at the type's 50th birthday party—scenes reminiscent of the massive airborne operations in World War 2 such as Arnhem and D-Day. [*Norman Pealing*]

BELOW *The Tinker Belle* is the CAF's magnificent Curtiss C-46 Commando, a machine which demands 'hands on' attention from the pilots at all times. [*Norman Pealing*]

LEFT Despite the streamlined shape of the fuselage extending over the nose (the hull was originally designed for pressurization), visibility from the flight deck is very good. The C-46 did a fantastic trucking job over the 'Hump' route from India to China across the Himalayas in World War 2, braving 20,000 foot peaks and 100 mph headwinds. [*Norman Pealing*]

RIGHT Of ample proportions, the C-46 is nevertheless an attractive aircraft. About 3300 were delivered between October 1941 and VJ-Day. [*Norman Pealing*]

GOOD GUYS

Douglas A-26 Invader pictured at Oshkosh in 1984 – complete with machine-guns that could be heard firing blanks in flight. The real thing packed up to 16 0.50 caliber weapons during World War 2 and Korea. [*Nigel Moll*]

The Casper, Wyoming-based Tired Iron Racing Team brought their B-26C Invader *Puss & Boots* to Reno in 1985 and unexpectedly gained a starting position in the Unlimited Bronze race, where Mike Wright cruised the big bomber to sixth place at 283.96 mph. Discovered in the early 1980s in a derelict condition in Brazil, this Invader was bought by the Tired Iron team and Mike and Dick Wright traveled to Brazil, where they spent months bringing the old bird back to life. The brothers put the aircraft into flyable shape with the addition of two new R-2800s and lots of labor. This aircraft had served

with the *Forca Aerea Brasileira* and was one of the
Invaders modified by Hamilton Aircraft in Arizona,
but after passing from active service, the airframe was
basically abandoned. Fortunately, the ferry flight
back to the States went smoothly and the Invader's
restoration was completed. [*Mike Jerram*]

LEFT In tight formation are two of the exotic warbirds in the Confederate Air Force's remarkable collection. On the left is the P-39 Airacobra in Soviet Air Force markings, reflecting the fact that nearly half of those built were provided to the Soviet Union under Lend Lease during World War 2; leading is an A-20 Havoc, Douglas's hard-working and highly successful low-level bomber of World War 2, also known as the Boston by the RAF. [*Philip Handleman*]

BELOW, MAIN PICTURE The CAF's B-17 Flying Fortress *Texas Raiders* thunders overhead at the 'Confederate' airshow at Harlingen, 1987. If there is one single aircraft that captures public imagination when bombers of World War 2 are discussed, then that aircraft is the Boeing B-17 Flying Fortress. [*Philip Handleman*]

BELOW, INSET A close-up of the Fort's fine nose art. *Texas Raiders* plays a big part in the reenactment program at Rebel Field. [*Philip Handleman*]

GOOD GUYS

The Confederate Air Force Flying Fortress *Sentimental Journey* brings some grace to the Reno races of 1982. When obtained by the Arizona Wing of the CAF the B-17G was without turrets, but diligent work by the CAF has seen all three restored to the airframe. The fine condition of *Sentimental Journey*, probably the most authentically restored Fortress still flying, is due entirely to dedicated volunteer workers. [*Nigel Moll*]

BAD GUYS

LEFT The business end of the CAF's CASA-built He-111 bomber: the glazed nose confered superb visibility for the pilot and bomb-aimer cum gunner in good weather, but made them vulnerable to head-on attacks by fighters. [*Mike Jerram*]

BELOW The Heinkel's copilot prepares to 'lock in' the greenhouse cockpit of this classic bomber. [*Norman Pealing*]

LEFT AND BELOW Luftwaffe fly-by at the CAF airshow in 1987: a Messerschmitt Me-108 Taifun flies wing on the CASA 2111. The shapely Taifun served with the Luftwaffe and German Army as a liaison and courier aircraft and was the percursor to the famous Bf-109 fighter. The He-111 was the first modern bomber to enter Luftwaffe service, its 200 mph-plus top speed leading Hermann Goering to conclude erroneously that it might outrun interceptors. The 111s which spearheaded the Blitz from 1940 were thus poorly defended and fell easy prey to RAF Hurricanes and Spitfires in daylight. But while it remained vulnerable to fighter attack, the He-111 was generally highly regarded as a flying machine, possessing few vices that mattered and being pleasant to handle, remaining in production in Germany until 1944. More than 7000 were built, including 200 111Hs by CASA in Spain, whose last production CASA 2111 left the factory as late as 1956. This airplane, powered by a pair of Rolls-Royce Merlins in place of the original Daimler-Benz or Junkers Jumo engines, was ferried to England in 1978 and later sold to the Confederate Air Force at Harlingen, Texas. CASA switched to the Rolls-Royce Merlin engine after supplies of the Junkers Jumo 2111F-2 dried up after 1945.
[*Photographs by Norman Pealing*]

LEFT A beautifully restored Junkers Ju-52, Germany's three-engined bomber popularly known as the Teutonic 'Tin Goose', captured at Oshkosh in 1984. [*Nigel Moll*]

BELOW Thick section high-lift wing with full-span ailerons and slotted flaps characterize the Ju-52/3M. The Junkers-developed 'double wing' concept bestowed remarkable STOL performance and slow flight capability on the aircraft, but could be troublesome in bad weather when ice tended to accumulate in the gap between the surfaces – leading to rapid loss of control. The corrugated airframe (**below right**) had legendary strength: one Luftwaffe pilot allegedly landed his *Tante Ju* on a tree-lined road and taxied for two miles, smashing down trees to clear a path for following aircraft. [*Mike Jerram*]

ABOVE 'Why does that airplane look like that, Mummy?' 'Because it's old and wrinkled like me.' No, they were built that way, earning the Junkers JU-52/3M tri-motor transport the well-deserved nickname *Iron Annie*. This corrugated wonder is actually a Spanish-built CASA 352. Some 170 *Tante Jus* were manufactured in Spain and remained in service until the 1970s, when the survivors were eagerly snapped up by warbird collectors. Englishman Doug Arnold owns five, including this one, and has a hangarful of spares for the flying Nissen huts. [*Mike Jerram*]

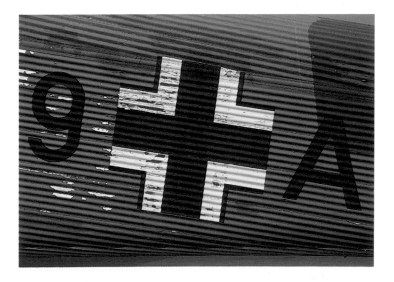

BAD GUYS

BELOW The Confederate Air Force's ex-Spanish Air Force HA.1112 Buchón (a license-built Bf-109G) makes the same noise as a Spitfire because it too has a Rolls-Royce Merlin up front. CASA-built 109s shared the awkward sideways-opening heavily framed canopy of the G Model (as here), but many were fitted with clear-vision Galland hoods. Interestingly, CAF pilots were contracted to fly these 109 lookalikes in the epic motion picture *The Battle of Britain*, made in 1968. [*Norman Pealing*]

RIGHT AND OPPOSITE, TOP Although more than 33,000 were built, no genuine German-manufactured Messerschmitt Bf-109 survives in airworthy condition. This imposter, owned by the Confederate Air Force, is a Spanish-built Hispano HA-1112 powered by a British-built Rolls-Royce Merlin engine. Some 28 HA-1112s were gathered together for the film *The Battle of Britain* and many have since

been dispersed among museums and private collections in England and the United States. The CAF has four of them, this one bearing the markings of a Luftwaffe unit serving on the Eastern Front. [*Mike Jerram*]

BOTTOM Carl Bücker's classic aerobatic Jungmeister biplane is best remembered as the mont of Count Otto von Hagenburg, Alex Papana, Jose Aresti and Prince Constantin Cantacuzene, but it was also used by the Luftwaffe for pilot training. Perfectly harmonized controls, with fingertip response so light and precise that any manouver could be started or stopped with pinpoint exactness, made the Jungmeister ideal for sharpening the reflexes of aspiring fighter-pilots, and much prized among collectors today. This example, flying in England, is unusual in having a Luftwaffe *Jagdfliegershule* color scheme. [*Mike Jerram*]

BAD GUYS

BELOW Only to be seen flying at Rebel Field with the Confederate Air Force is this delightful Focke Wulf Fw 44 Stieglitz, a biplane developed in 1932 as a primary and aerobatic trainer for the Luftwaffe. This beautiful machine is believed to be the world's only airworthy example. [*Norman Pealing*]

ABOVE The Fieseler Storch (this one is a French-built Morane MS.500) was another slow flier which could manage a near hover in a modest breeze. Difficult to fly, with little natural stability and poorly harmonized controls, the Storch was nonetheless a remarkable performer in capable hands. Indeed SS Hauptsturmführer Otto Skorzeny organized a rescue mission for the Italian dictator Benito Mussolini in September 1943 using a Storch to pluck *Il Duce* from incarceration on a peak of the Gran Sasso Massif, more than 9000 feet up and accessible only by cable-car: the Storch landed on a 200-yard rock-strewn strip on the side of the mountain. French-built aircraft like this one switched to metal-framed wings rather than wood after occupying Germans discovered French patriots sabotaging the aircraft by relieving themselves into the glue which held the wings together ... [*Mike Jerram*]

BELOW This Fleet Finch trainer is not so rare as the Stieglitz next door, but it's still a rare bird. As the markings suggest, a few saw RAF service between the world wars. [*Norman Pealing*]

BAD GUYS

BELOW *Tora! Tora! Tora!* Replica *Kate* torpedo bombers begin their dive as they approach airshow center at Rebel Field in 1987. One of the highlights at the annual CAF airshow is the dramatic recreation of the Japanese attack on Pearl Harbor. As the make-believe attackers rush by on their first bomb run, pyrotechnics experts on the ground detonate flame-producing explosives that throw swirling smoke into the air. Wave after wave of the mock invaders follow, swooping down and pulling up, quickly filling the blackened sky. It's controlled pandemonium, unlike any other airshow performance, and the vast crowd loves it. [*Philip Handleman*]

RIGHT Replica *Zeros* circle their target—a predesignated spot in front of and safely distant from the airshow audience. [*Philip Handleman*]

RIGHT The swordfish looks about ready to go, but of course it remains firmly latched. [*Philip Handleman*]

TEAMWORK

No airshow would be complete without jet aerobatics. And, not to be outdone by the mighty United States military air demonstration teams, the Canadian Armed Forces display their excellent team, the Snowbirds, at more than 60 shows throughout North America. Seen here are all nine members engaged in an aerial ballet at the Freedom Festival Air Show in Windsor, Ontario, in 1987. [*Philip Handleman*]

ABOVE LEFT AND LEFT The team's nine Canadair Tutors are relatively slow and low-powered, but those qualities are no handicap when combined with Snowbird choreography – on display here at Reno 82, when they performed 23 different manouvers including five-abreast loops and rolls. [*Nigel Moll*]

ABOVE The nine-aircraft formation passes gracefully, the symmetry of the lingering smoke trails restating the extent of the team members' skill.
[*Philip Handleman*]

LEFT The precision of the USAF's Thunderbirds Air Demonstration Squadron is evidenced by this line-abreast climb. It's almost as if some invisible puppeteer is pulling strings to keep all the F-16 Fighting Falcon multi-role fighters in exact position. [*Philip Handleman*]

RIGHT After an awesome display, a team member taxies before an approving audience. The military air demonstration teams signify something special during the airshow season. They are the no-nonsense performers who command the hottest machines in the sky, and when they perform at a show, no one leaves until they have finished. [*Philip Handleman*]

BELOW During a tight diamond formation the Thunderbirds display the patriotic paint scheme on their upper fuselages and tails. Mounted on the F-16 since 1982, the team has previously utilized the F-84 Thunderstreak, F-100 Super Sabre, F-105 Thunderchief, F-4 Phantom and T-38 Talon. [*Philip Handleman*]

ABOVE LEFT While rolled to knife-edge flight, the 'thunderbird' motif painted on the underside is easily recognizable. The US Air Force chose this theme for its air demonstration team because according to American Indian lore the bird possesses the ability to produce thunder – an ability sought by fighter-pilots. [*Philip Handleman*]

LEFT Helping to celebrate the 40th anniversary of Chuck Yeager's conquering of the speed of sound, the US Air Force's Thunderbirds produce a wondrously symmetrical shape against the crystal clear sky over Edwards Air Force Base during a 1987 airshow. [*Philip Handleman*]

ABOVE The Thunderbirds make a delta pass, looking more like a single coordinated machine than six separate entities, each with its own pilot in command. [*Philip Handleman*]

LEFT Blue Angels on echelon parade in their new F/A-18 Hornets at the Willow Run Air Show in Michigan during the 1987 season. [*Philip Handleman*]

BELOW LEFT Like their Air Force counterparts, the US Navy's Blue Angels travel across the country wowing airshow crowds. Here they are seen in their tight diamond formation. [*Philip Handleman*]

BELOW Stacked like pancakes! Only a few feet apart, four crack naval aviators offer yet another flying definition of the word precision. [*Philip Handleman*]

TEAMWORK

The Canadian Snowbirds provide an elegant symbol of comradeship in the sky. Their trusty mount, the indigenous CT-114 Tutor, is a reliable old basic jet trainer. [*Philip Handleman*]